MW01224041

LEARNING MANDARIN CHINESE

BEGINNER'S LEVEL

A simple and easy way to learn
Mandarin Chinese in the 21st century

DEUTSCH SHACHAR

Learning Mandarin Chinese

Beginner's Level

A simple and easy way to learn Mandarin Chinese in the 21ˢᵗ century

Author: Deutsch Shachar

Language consulting and proofreading: Chen Xiaofei 陈晓飞

Dedicated to future generations…

Table of Contents

Author's notes

In this book, a great deal of thought has been invested in how the Western world's citizens in the 21st century could start to understand the Asian world better. This thought is so far geographically, culturally, and linguistically particularly in the Chinese world.

The book is a result of many years of experience on how to effectively learn the Chinese language and do it smartly while studying the language and Chinese culture at Tel-Aviv University's East Asian Department, and the years after until today.

The lecturers and teachers of the East Asian Studies department invested a lot in their students to allow them to experience the Chinese culture in its best way, starting from lectures on historical introduction to telling the history of East Asia in general and that of China in particular, and so on with modern Chinese language, spoken (Mandarin dialect) and written (Simplified and a bit of Traditional Chinese Characters).

This book is dedicated to everyone eager or alternately interested in learning the Chinese language quickly, efficiently, with fun, and at ease. After a little taste of the language, as you could see from reading and practicing this book, so much similar to tasting a bit from some delicious Chinese food, I guess you will probably not only like to continue learning the language but also continue with my next book that teaches on how to write the simplified modern Chinese characters.

Let's move on to our first introduction to learn this inspirational and fascinating Chinese language. I wish you all to enjoy your quest!

Introduction to Learning the Chinese Language

The Chinese language is not as it seems to be... Does it seem to you as a **difficult and complicated** language to learn?

What if I told you that it is one of the **easiest** languages to learn by speaking and writing, only in the sole condition of knowing how to learn it. Would you still like to know why it is an easy language and as a consequence, you will be interested to know more?

As a teacher, who teaches Chinese in Mandarin dialect, I try to find new methods, techniques, and simple ways of learning the Chinese language, which will be super-efficient and hopefully easier than blind memorization of Chinese words and grammatical rules. The truth is that I dedicate most of my time to this issue. By doing so, I try to show you and raise your awareness on how much this language is interesting and even **quite beneficial** for certain aspects in your daily-life nowadays, in the 21st century.

12 years ago, in my undergraduate studies for B. A in East Asian Studies at Tel-Aviv University, I started to "fall in love" more and more with this language and its culture.

The Chinese language seemed then and still seems today as one of the **most vital languages to humans on earth**. The language is not only vital & important now, but also in the future. Nowadays, it is not a secret that it's been a few decades since China "opened itself to the world" and is developing at the speed of light, influencing us in a great manner - culturally, educationally, and financially, among other aspects.

Suppose we start with our session learning about the Chinese language. In that case, we will notice that there are many different dialects. Among them, Mandarin and Cantonese are the most famous, well-known, and most common ones in China mainland.

Every time I say "Chinese language" in this book, I will refer to the Mandarin dialect. The main languages that will be notified in this book will be **Chinese** (Mandarin) and **Cantonese**. Chinese is usually the reference for the Mandarin dialect. Since Mandarin is the official dialect and the spoken language of the People's Republic of China (PRC), I will **refer** to China here in our book.

If we go back and look at China from a historical view, this great Chinese civilization has focused in the same geographical place over the globe for 5,000 years (more or less). This civilization assisted the human race to develop and educate itself in many aspects of life, starting at developing new products throughout history such as **Paper**, **Gun Powder**, the **Compass**, and continuing in developing different perceptions, points of view and philosophies regarding Human, Nature, the Universe and their reciprocal relations respectively.

If we take a deeper look into this diverse culture, we could notice that the spoken language structure and the wisdom that sets behind it is really interesting since it does not only serve as a language that **separates complex words into their simple parts**, as we will see later in the book, but the spoken language is also a kind of **melody or music** when spoken by Chinese speakers. This "music" finds its way among billions of people every day.

In Mandarin, we have **four different tones** (tone is a pronunciation of a syllable in a specific intonation), while the tones can be one of the following: steady elevated tone called "Tone 1" / "First tone," raising tone called "Tone 2" / "Second tone," down and raising tone which is also called "Tone 3" / "Third tone" and sharp down tone called "Tone 4" / "Fourth tone." We will expand and explain more on this issue later in this book.

To sum it up, it is clear that the goal of this book is sharp and straight-forward, which is to show the readers how easy, interesting, and important it is to start and even continue learning the Chinese language while learning from the foundations in a precise and in an efficient way.

This book contains **groups of vocabulary** in different aspects and daily life situations while being organized in a grammatical way, such as common nouns, adjectives, adverbs, verbs, phrase templates, etc. Important grammar points and many exercises and practice are also given to ensure you start speaking Chinese in the most standard way and as soon as possible.

The western Romanization technique (Romanization is when writing a foreign language in Latin letters), which is also the way a lot of western people began to learn the Chinese Language called **PinYin** (Literally in Chinese: "Spelling by Sound").

PinYin is, as noted above, **a Romanization technique** that uses the Latin alphabet to pronounce the Chinese written language / Chinese characters. While doing so, the tones (the 4 tones mentioned above) are being marked in **PinYin tone marks** above the syllable's vowels, so we consequently could speak like a Chinese speaker with the right tones.

This issue of tones is very different from the western languages (languages in the west only have intonation of a sentence, not each word that the tone actually sets the meaning of the word!). This **PinYin Romanization transcript system** and as I will mention it here in this book – this **"mid-language"** (a mediate language between English and Chinese), will serve us a lot in learning spoken Chinese, which is our main tool for reaching this awesome language.

Pronunciation, Tones, and PinYin – Further explained

Mandarin Chinese (PRC's official language) is constructed from **4 tones**. As we have mentioned before, English has no tones for words that set their meaning, and by that, it is difficult sometimes to grasp the tones at the start of the learning process. Don't worry, the explanation will be thorough and clear as possible.

The 4 tones will guide us **in which manner to say the words** in Chinese language. For example, if we have two identical one-syllable words **('ma' and 'ma')** but in different tones **('mā' and 'mǎ')**, each syllable will be a different word with a different meaning, and consequently, they will be **different words**.

The meaning of the Chinese word `'mā'` is **'Mom'** in English. The meaning of the Chinese word **'mǎ'** is **'Horse'** in English. Obviously, *it is critical* to know the tones in Mandarin so that we don't refer to our mom as a horse...

Another funny example is creating two different words by adding the identical one-syllable word **'Tang'** one-time **tone number 1 / the 1st tone** and adding **Tone number 2 / the 2nd tone** the other time. In this case, **'Tāng'** in Mandarin means **'Soup'** in English, while the word **'Táng'** in Mandarin actually means **'Sugar'** in English.

This example above reminds me of an old funny Chinese story about a Foreigner who entered a restaurant in China to ask for a soup. The waiter, a polite Chinese person, who tried to decipher the foreigner's accent and meaning of the word, smiled and respected the foreigner by going to the kitchen and gave him his weird request of a bowl full of **sugar**…

Here, we can see how much we need and really should pay attention to tones in Chinese language so the Chinese people could **understand us correctly**. Actually, by speaking Chinese and practicing it more than once or twice, with Chinese people or with advanced Chinese language speakers, you will notice that when you pronounce the tone of words in a wrong way or like a beginner in the language, it could result in a surprise understanding of the right meaning by the Chinese person which is due to the speed of the Mandarin speaker.

This happens because the Chinese people use **Context** to understand the meaning of words and things during conversations. Understanding things out of context and not in an "out of context" manner is part of Chinese' people's point of view reflected in the Chinese language, as we can see here.

In my opinion, Mandarin Chinese tones add some "flavoring and seasoning" to the language. Therefore, Chinese people are consequently speaking a language full of life and vitality, which we see also in the culture reflected in Chinese paintings. In Chinese art, the *flow and vitality* of shapes are not less important than the painting's content itself.

We are now aware that the ancient Chinese designed the language to be lively and not "boring." Only a few people sitting near a Chinese group or next to a few Chinese people in the restaurant, eating and chatting, can hear the flow and liveliness of the sounds of the language expressed by the 4 tones by those Chinese people. It seems that sometimes every small or large group of Chinese has its own "musical party."

In **Table 1**, you can see the sound scales of the 4 tones. **The 1st tone** is flat and located on the high-pitch level. **The 2nd tone** is moving from the mid-pitch level to the high-pitch level gradually. **The 3rd tone** is located in the mid-pitch level (more or less), going down to the low-pitch level and changing its trend towards the high-pitch level. And finally, **the 4th tone** is located on the high-pitch level and sharply going down to the low-pitch level.

Table 1: The 4 Tones in Mandarin Chinese

If we move a second from the **sounds of the language** to **how the PinYin is constructed**, we could see that the Chinese words in PinYin are constructed from 2 parts: Initials & Finals.

Initials are the part that starts the syllable/word (if the word is a one-syllable word), and **Finals** are the part that ends it.

In **Table 2,** the **initials and finals** are presented on how to pronounce them in English (even though PinYin uses the Latin Alphabet, **30%-40%** (more or less) are being pronounced differently than in English).

Explanation on how to pronounce each initial and final is therefore being provided. The letters that are being pronounced differently are marked here in yellow for your convenience.

Note: when we have the letter 'G' only at the end of a word in PinYin, the letter will have a swollen sound, like it is barely pronounced.

Table 2: Initials & Finals in PinYin & English Pronunciation

Initials

b	p	m	f	d	t	n	l
g	k	h	j	q	x	zh	ch
sh	r	z	c	s	y	w	

Finals

a	o	e	i	u	ü	ai	ei
ui	ao	ou	iu	ie	ue	er	an
en	in	un	ün	ang	eng	ing	ong

PinYin	English		PinYin	English		PinYin	English
H =	H (from the Throat)		ZH =	dge		Ü =	sound, like 'u' that are being spoken by a French person (two cheeks pushed inside the mouth)
J =	dzi		R =	jea/r			
Q =	tsi		Z =	dz			
X =	see		C =	ts			

13

Practicing on connecting the Initials & Finals to a syllable

and pronouncing it accordingly in PinYin

Awesome! Now let's connect the two parts (Initials & Finals) to a single syllable and read it aloud. It is evident in the vocabulary shown in the rest of the book that many words in Chinese **consist of a single syllable**. After this practice in **Table 3**, we will add the tones we mentioned before. Then the syllables will turn into **meaningful words!** Splendid! So what are we waiting for then?! Let's start:

Table 3: Practicing on connecting Initials and Finals

Pinyin Pronunciation	English Pronunciation
Bao	Bau
Mao	Mau
Feng	Fang
Tian	Tien
Nan	Nan
Lian	Lien
Zang	Dzang
Cao	Tsau
Su	Su
Zhang	Dgeng
Cha	Cha
Shuang	Shuang
Ren	Jren
Jin	Dzin
Qiang	Tsiang
Xin	Seen
Gao	Gau
Kong	Kong
Hao	Hau
Hui	Hwei

Tones – explanation and practice

We will place our <u>PinYin tone marks</u> above the next vowels:

a, e, i, o, u, ü.   (----> for example: ā, ě, ǐ, ō, ú, ǔ.)

In PinYin, there is <u>no rule regarding the vowels above to place the tone mark (1st, 2nd, 3rd or 4th tone) if there are</u> 2 vowels one after the other.

For example, suppose we have the PinYin syllable 'Mian.' In that case, if I don't know what this word means or if I haven't studied it yet, <u>I would not know where to put the tone mark</u> – will it be placed above the vowel 'i' or 'a', there is really no rule to know. Therefore, **<u>only after learning the syllable with its tone mark</u>** (which means I have studied the <u>word or part of the word,</u> which usually consists of two-three syllables) **I would know for sure**. For example, the syllable is actually a word that means **'Face.'** The tone mark above the **'a'** vowel (in this case, it will be the 4th tone) and therefore will look like **'Miàn.'**

The tone marks in the syllable **'Men'** look like the following: the first tone will be 'Mēn.' The second tone will be 'Mén.' The third tone will be 'Měn.' The fourth tone will be 'Mèn.' There is also a neutral tone (sometimes there are people who like to call it "zero tone"). The neutral tone will be marked **<u>with a dot</u>** in PinYin **before the syllable**. For example, the neutral tone in 'Men' will look like

'.**Men**'. This book will start with a dot for the zero tone and <u>will</u> <u>continue gradually without it.</u>

There are also rules for connecting tones – for example, two words with 3rd tone each become two words that the first word has a <u>2nd</u> <u>tone and the later has a 3rd tone</u>, such as the following example here:

Hěn Hǎo -------> Hén Hǎo

The two words in English mean **"Very good."**

We will learn these few rules a bit later in this book because I would like you first to be a bit familiarized with the PinYin system and its tones.

<u>So we can summarize it all and say that:</u>

* **Initial + Final** = Syllable

* **One/two/three syllables + Tone** = A word in Chinese

So let's practice a bit by combining a few syllables (initials + finals) with tones and see what words in **PinYin** will come out:

* n + i + 3rd tone ------------------> **nǐ**   **nǐ** = means the word 'You'

* h + ao + 3rd tone ----------------> **hǎo**   **hǎo** = means the word 'Good'

* sh + ao + 3rd tone -----> **shǎo**   **shǎo** = means the word 'A little'

* m + en + 2nd tone --------> **mén**   **mén** = means the word 'Door'; 'Gate'

* f + an + 4th tone ---------> **fàn**   **fàn** = means the word 'Food'; 'Rice'

* g + ao + 1st tone ---------> **gāo**   **gāo** = means the word 'Tall'; 'High'

After explaining the tones, the initials and the finals, which all contribute to making a word in Mandarin, we can now continue learning the Chinese language with the aid of this "mid-language" that we are now know and call **PinYin**. As said before, PinYin literally means "Spelling by Sound" (**Pīn = 'to spell'   Yīn = 'sound').**

Together, it is called **PīnYīn**. Now you understand why it looks like this, with two flat lines above the 2 syllables -----> it is the tone marks that completes the result of **a word with the right meaning**! Let's continue then.

The next thing is that we will start to learn the chapters with **vocabulary**, **grammar points**, **texts** and all kinds of **exercises** to practice what we learn. At the end of each chapter, answers to the exercises will be waiting for you.

At the beginning of each chapter, you will be shown daily life vocabulary in different topics and situations. By this, you could "taste" a bit from every basic practical topic, more than other books or dictionaries that just "throw over" to you with a mass of information that is actually not so effective for understanding and implementing at that moment or later on.

Have a coffee break, rest, and come back **fully charged** with energy to our next chapter. See you in chapter 1!

Picture 1: Chinese people eating traditional Hotpot meal at a local restaurant in Shanghai, China.

Chapter 1

Starting the Day

A. Vocabulary

Times		Verbs	
Zǎoshàng	Early morning	Chī	To eat
Xiàwǔ	Afternoon	Hē	To drink
Wǎnshàng	evening		
Měitiān	Every day		

		Nouns	
		Kāfēi	Coffee
Pronouns		Shuǐ	Water
Wǒ	I; Me	Fàn	Food; Rice
Nǐ	You		
Tā	He; She; It	Adverbs	
		Bù	No

Question Words		Conjunctions	
.ma	Particle expressing a question	Hé	And

B. Grammar

1. Basic sentence structure

Each sentence in Chinese usually starts from the most basic structure composed of the following parts:

Subject + (Adverb) + Verb + Object

Therefore, these 3 parts (optional 4 parts)* are the foundations of the Chinese language, which is composed of the most basic sentence structure compound. This basic structure is probably the most important thing you need to remember in Chinese Grammar! After remembering this structure, your life will be much **easier** because all the sentence structures in Chinese and the grammar part are added on top of this structure. Chinese Grammar is modular, and therefore the study of Chinese Grammar is gradual and consistent. We will see all of this in the next grammar points in this chapter and the following chapters.

* Note: the **Adverb** is optional and, therefore, in many basic sentences will not be used. At the start of our learning process, I put it here to make future learning in this book as easier.

* Explanation of basic sentence structure:

Subject – the thing/person that the sentence is talking about.

Adverb – the part that describes the verb – **how** the action was made or **not** made, made **too much**, etc.

Verb – the verb is the action that the subject is doing.

Object – the thing/person that on it/him/her the action is being made – to eat **rice**, to drink **coffee,** etc.

2. Basic sentence + time structure

As shown in B.1 above, other parts are being added modularly, like the Lego game for kids, on top of the basic sentence structure. In this case, we are adding **time** to the sentence.

For example, if we take the time duration "morning" and put it into the basic sentence structure, we will put it at the beginning of the sentence; most of the **time, it will come before the subject.**

This is how the **new** sentence will look like with **time phrase** added to it:

Time + Subject + (Adverb) + Verb + Object

C. Exercises

Practicing the new vocabulary together with the new grammar points

So, we have **vocabulary** and have **2 sentence structures** that we can now use – so let's start putting together some sentences in Chinese!!! I know you are thrilled (:

C.1. Sentence translation

Please translate the following English sentences into Chinese PinYin. (The 2 first sentences are already translated as example sentences)

* Please pay special attention to the vocabulary and the sentence structures. It is recommended to read the translated sentence aloud to yourself when you translate the English sentences. Hence, you start getting familiar with the Mandarin Chinese tones.

   a. Every day (in the) morning, I drink coffee.

      _____

   b. In the evening I eat rice.

      _____

   c. Afternoon, I drink water.

_____

d. He drinks water and coffee.

_____

e. Afternoon, I don't drink coffee.

_____

f. In the morning, do you drink coffee?

_____

g. Afternoon, I eat food and drink water.

_____

h. In the morning, do you drink tea(female)?

_____

i. Every day in the evening, I drink water.

_____

j. In the evening, I don't drink coffee.

_____

* Important reminder:

At the end of each chapter, the chapter's answers for the exercises will be made available for you.

C.2. Text

Měitiān zǎoshàng wǒ hē kāfēi. Xiàwǔ wǒ hē shuǐ hé chī fàn.

Wǎnshàng wǒ bù hē kāfēi. Nǐ měitiān zǎoshàng hē shuǐ ma?

Tā měitiān zǎoshàng hē shuǐ ma?

* Please try to translate the Text from Chinese PinYin into English:

_____

_____

_____

_____

_____

D. Chapter summary

At the end of this chapter, you already know some vocabulary in Chinese and some grammar points. You have translated sentences from Chinese (PinYin) into English.

Folks, you are **only at the end of the first chapter** and you already know how to communicate in Mandarin Chinese!!! Think of how much you could progress with the next chapters ahead. I'm really proud of you and I hope you will continue to enjoy and **succeed big time!**

From here, we will continue ahead in **full power,** enriching ourselves with the Chinese language. **Remember!** The Chinese language <u>is an art</u>. Treat it like that, and it will reward you accordingly.

E. The culture corner

The traditional Chinese fishermen

The traditional Chinese fisherman takes a simple but steady bamboo boat, sailing on top of the river water. At the same time, he uses the **Cormorant** bird to catch fish.The cormorants are specialized in diving into the river and catch fish. They bring the fish to the Chinese fisherman and go back to the water for the next fish.

Chinese fishers use this ancient fishing method by taming those birds and achieve harmonious cooperation with nature.

Picture 2: Chinese Fisherman in Li River at Guilin, China.

Answers to chapter 1

C.1. Sentence translation

a. Xiàwǔ wǒ hē shuǐ.

b. Tā hē shuǐ hé kāfēi.

c. Xiàwǔ wǒ bù hē kāfēi.

d. Zǎoshàng nǐ hē kāfēi .ma?

e. Xiàwǔ wǒ chī fàn hé hē shuǐ.

f. Zǎoshàng nǐ hē chá ma?

g. Měitiān wǎnshàng wǒ hē shuǐ.

h. Wǎnshàng wǒ bù hē kāfēi.

C.2. Text

Every day in the morning, I drink coffee. In the afternoon, I drink water and eat rice/food. In the evening, I don't drink coffee. Do you drink coffee every day in the morning? Does he drink coffee every day in the morning?

Chapter 2

Ordering food at the restaurant

A. Vocabulary:

Times		Verbs	
Zhōngwǔ	Noon	Gěi	To give
.De shí.hou	While / When (doing something)	Diǎn	To order (a dish)
Yèlǐ	Night	Qù	To go
jīntiān	Today	Qǐng	To ask / to invite somebody to somewhere
		Yào	To want / To need
Pronouns			
Wǒmén	We		
Nǐmén	You (Plural)		
Tāmén	They	**Nouns**	
		Cài	A dish
		Kuàizi	Chopsticks
		Mǐfàn	Cooked rice
Adverbs		Chá	Tea
		Wǎn	Bowl
Yě	Also (comes before a verb)	Tāng	Soup
Dōu	All / Everyone / Everything / In all cases	Cānguǎn	Restaurant

Measure words		Numbers	
Wǎn	MW for bowls	Yī	One
Bēi	MW for cups	Èr	Two (ordinal number)
Shuāng	MW for pairs	Sān	Three
Gè	General MW	Liǎng	Two (for counting)

B. Grammar:

The time order in the Chinese language and culture goes **from the big to the small**, from the **macro to the micro.** This is a Chinese philosophical perception. We have to know it when learning and engaging the Chinese language. Therefore, when we build a Chinese sentence with a **time phrase,** we will always start from the bigger time phrase to the smaller one.

For instance, the <u>date format</u> as it is customary in the English language is **February 8th, 2020**.

29

In Chinese language, the bigger time phrase or time duration here is the **Year**, after that, it is the **Month,** and after that, it is the **Day**.

Therefore we will build the date as follows:

Year 2020, Month February, Day 8th.

For instance, a specific time in the week will be as follows:

Sunday, Morning, 7 am.

In illustration 2, we can see a visual example of the dimensions of time order.

illustration 2:
The Chinese Philosophical Perception- From Macro Size to Micro Size, as expressed for example in time perception in Chinese language Grammar.

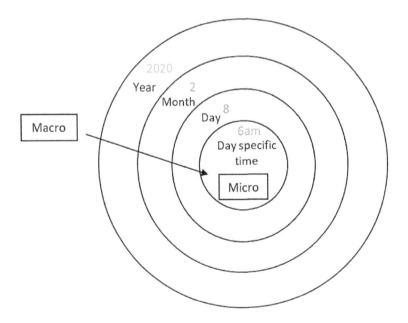

2. Measure words:

There is a philosophical perception in the Chinese culture that is also a religion called **Daoism** (or Taoism). This point of view observes the universe and nature and tries to learn their ways and patterns. **Daoism** is also trying to divide the different parts and phenomena into **different categories**. Those categories are being found in nature in the cosmic order and therefore should be learned by us, humans.

For example, some wise Chinese Daoists looking at how water flows in nature – starting from the river and finally washing to the sea, looking at nature's different phenomena such as erosion and construction, looking at the life cycle of animals, and the way they behave, etc.

The Measure Words absorbs their value from this Dao point of view in a matter that these words **separate nouns and characteristics of processes in nature into**

different categories so they could be seen and organized as features of that cosmic order.

In our language learning case, **Measure Words are words that separate nouns into different categories while counting objects.** For example, the categories can be round things, flat things, things with handles, **things that look like a stick**, etc.

Therefore, if we would like, for instance, to count 2 tables, **in English we will say "two tables,"** but in Chinese, we will count the two tables and then associate them with the category of flat Things, so in this case, **it will be referred in Chinese as "two** flat **tables."**

We will learn some Measure Words (or Counting Words, or Category Words) in each chapter, and we will get to know them through our learning process in this book. It is important to say that in the process of learning these Measure Words, or in short MW, we will need to memorize them each time.

Another important issue before we head to the Counting Formula structure is that when we can't remember or don't know the MW for a certain noun, we should always associate the noun and categorize it with the General MW, **which is 'gè.'**

3. The Counting Formula:

Every time we see these 3 parts in a sentence – **a number, a Measure Word** and a **Noun**, we shall refer to it as the **Counting Formula**. With this formula's aid, we will count things in Chinese language <u>by their category</u>, just like it was explained in the grammar point above.

For example, if we would like to say "one (pair of) pants," we will say **"one (pair of)** look like stick **pants."** In a similar case, we will say **"one** with handle **chair," "one** come in pairs **chopsticks,"** etc.

The Counting Formula looks as follows:

> Number + Measure Word + Noun

Examples of using the Counting Formula:

a. sān zhāng zhuōzi ---> 3 flat tables

b. yī tiáo kùzi ---> 1 stick like pants

C. Exercises

Practicing the new vocabulary together with the new grammar points:

So we have already briefly discussed chapter 2's vocabulary and have new fresh grammar points that we can use, so let's start practicing. This time we will start with an easy and fun exercise.

C.1. Word to picture matching

Please, take a look at the small pictures on the following page and associate the matching words in Chinese Pinyin from the word bank.

* <u>Word Bank</u>: Kuàizi, Cānguǎn, Wǎn, Mǐfàn, Tāng, Chá.

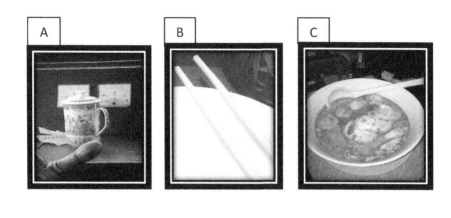

_____   _____   _____

_____   _____

_____

C.2. PīnYīn to English matching

Please match each word in English to its corresponding meaning in Chinese PīnYīn according to Chapter 2 vocabulary.

dōu	mw for bowls
sān	mw for cups
yī	mw for pairs
èr	also
yě	all; in all cases
wǎn	one
shuāng	two (ordinal number)
bēi	three
yào	two (for counting)
tāmén	while (doing something…)
liǎng	soup
.de shíhou	tea
Jīntiān	they
Tāng	to want/to need
Kuàizi	today
Chá	chopsticks

C.3. Sentence translation

Please translate the following English sentences into Chinese PinYin.

* Pay attention to the vocabulary and the sentence structures. It is recommended to read the translated sentences aloud to yourselves while translating the English sentences.

** For your convenience, important grammar points discussed above in this chapter are marked with color and *different font* sizes.

    a. I want to go to a restaurant.

    _____

    b. Please give me 3 bowls of rice and 1 cup (of) tea.

    _____

    c. We would like to order 3 cups (of) tea.

    _____

    d. Today in the afternoon, he will go to a restaurant.

    _____

    e. He doesn't want to order food.

    _____

    f. They don't want to order food?

    _____

g. They don't want to eat rice. They all want to drink tea.

_____

C.4. Text

Jīntiān zhōngwǔ wǒmen dōu qù cānguǎn. Wǒ yào diǎn yī wǎn mǐfàn. Nǐ yě yào diǎn mǐfàn ma? Wǒ yào diǎn yī bēi chá, tā yě yào diǎn yī bēi chá. Jīntiān wǒ, nǐ hé tā dōu yào qù cānguǎn, hē chá hé chī mǐfàn.

* Please try to translate the Text from Chinese PinYin into English:

_____

_____

_____

D. Chapter summary

In this chapter, we advanced a bit more in vocabulary and grammar. We realized that we could read and understand a text in Chinese PīnYīn. In the next chapter, we will start to get to know some Chinese friends, and we will learn how to introduce ourselves in a simple and quick way.

See you soon...

E. The culture corner

The harbor-city of Shànghǎi

The meaning of the name Shanghai is Shàng = on, Hǎi = sea. The city is called "on the sea" because it seats near the East-China Sea.

Shànghǎi is a harbor city in center-east China with a population of more than 25 million people!!! It is respectively one of the biggest and most important cities of China in the aspects of economy and development. Due to the foreign countries that came to the city in the 19th century, the importance of the city as a commercial center has increased and continues to rise until today.

In Shànghǎi, many districts are distinct in their character, architecture and atmosphere according to the foreign country which settled there in the past, respectively. For example, The French district is well designed with European architecture and many luxurious restaurants.

One of the city's main attractions is **The Bund**, a vast river line sitting on the west bank of the Huángpǔ River and being used as a promenade for the tourists who come to see the beauty of the city. From The Bund, one could see the skyline of the sky-scrapers on the east side of the Huángpǔ River. This area in the east of Huángpǔ River is called Pǔdōng and literally means "East from Pǔ." This area with its amazing skyline is one of the most associated symbols of the city, reflecting the city's massive and quick development in the past 30 years, which was a simple area of fishers and villages before.

Picture 3: A view to HSBC Building in The Bund, Shanghai, China.

Picture 4: A view to Shanghai's sky-scrapers laminated in different colors.

Answers for chapter 2

C.1. Word to picture matching

Picture A – chá. (tea)

Picture B – kuàizi. (chopsticks)

Picture C – tāng. (soup)

Picture D – cānguǎn. (restaurant)

Picture E – wǎn. (bowl)

Picture F – mǐfàn. (cooked rice)

C.2. PīnYīn to English matching

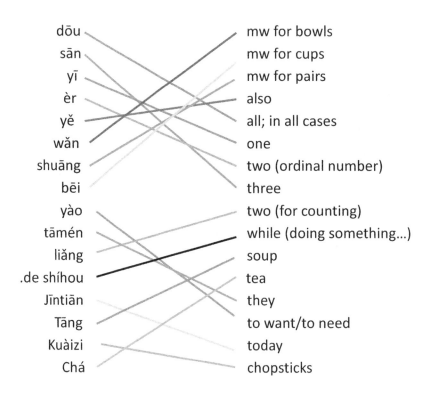

dōu	mw for bowls
sān	mw for cups
yī	mw for pairs
èr	also
yě	all; in all cases
wǎn	one
shuāng	two (ordinal number)
bēi	three
yào	two (for counting)
tāmén	while (doing something...)
liǎng	soup
.de shíhou	tea
Jīntiān	they
Tāng	to want/to need
Kuàizi	today
Chá	chopsticks

C.3. Sentence translation

i. Wǒ yào qù cānguǎn.

ii. Qǐng gěi wǒ sān wǎn mǐfàn hé yī bēi chá.

iii. Wǒmén yào diǎn sān bēi chá.

iv. Jīntiān Xiàwǔ tā qù cānguǎn.

v. Tā bù yào diǎn fàn.

vi. Tāmén bù yào diǎn fàn .ma?

vii. Tāmén bù yào chī mǐfàn, tāmén dōu yào hē chá.

C.4. Text

Today, at noon, we will all go to a restaurant. I want to order one bowl of rice/cooked rice. Would you also like to order rice/cooked rice? I would like to order one cup of tea. He would also like to order one cup of tea. Today, you and he/she all want to go to a restaurant, drink tea, and eat rice/cooked rice.

41

Chapter 3

Getting to know some Chinese friends

A. Vocabulary

Adjectives		Common Phrases	
Hǎo	Good	nǐhǎo	Hello
Bùcuò	Not bad	nǐhǎo .ma?	How are you?
		xièxie	Thank you
		Zuìjìn zěnme yàng?	How Is it recently?
		Hái kěyǐ	Still ok
Verbs		Lǎo yàngzi	Same same
		Nǐ gàn .ma?	What are you up to?
Shì	To be (am/is/are)		
Xué	To learn/To study		
Zhù	To live		
Gōngzuò	To work	**Nouns**	
Jiào	To be called		
Zài	To be located at	Zhōngguó	China
Gàn	To do	Rén	A person; People
Huì	Can (to know how to do something)	Rénmen	People (The public; Random people in the street)
		Fǎguó	France
		Déguó	Germany

		Bālí	Paris
Zhàoměi	A girl called Zhaomei	Luómā	Rome
Máodì	A boy called Maodi	Xuéshēng	A student
		Dàxué	University
		Gōngzuò	Work
Adverbs		Lǜshī	Lawyer
		Shìwùsuǒ	Business office
Méi	Past negation	gōngsī	Company
Háishi	Still; Or (in question form)	Fǎcān	French dish/food
Zhèngzài	Right now form (-ing)	Wèidào	Taste
		Míngzì	Name
		Yīngwén	English language
		Zhōngwén	Chinese language
Possessions		Fǎyǔ	French language
.De	Of (possession particle)	Yìdàlìyǔ	Italian language
Wǒ de	Mine		
Nǐ de	Yours	Measure Words	
Tā de	His/Hers/Its		
		Míng	MW for honorable positions (lawyers,

43

		doctors, etc.)
Prepositions		**Auxiliary Verbs**
Zài	At; In; On	
		Zài	Expressing actions in progress (-ing)

B. Grammar:

1. Chinese names

In Chinese names, the family name comes before the given name. Chinese people see a great deal towards their name, reflecting their personality for that moment in their life and expressing their self-respect. Therefore, it is common in Chinese culture that people give themselves a different name relevant to them at that moment. This issue comes from **Confucianism**, which says it is important to have a name that reflects the person's character and individuality. It is a changing element in a person's life. Adopting a different western name by Chinese youngsters every few years is a very common phenomenon nowadays.

2. Possession

To make **possession** of an object to a person, we use the word '.De' after the person.

For example: 'mine' will be literally 'me of' in Chinese ------> wǒ .de.

If I want to say "my dog", I will literally say "me of dog", which will be **wǒ .de gǒu (dog).**

For close possession, like family members and home, '.De' is not needed due to the understanding of the close connection already.

3. The word 'wén' and its different meanings

The word 'wen' represents **two important meanings** in Chinese. The first meaning is **'language,'** and the other is **'culture.'** By that, we can see the close and inevitable connection between language and culture in Chinese society since ancient times. The culture is shaped by the language and vice versa. Suppose the Chinese language is the "mirror" of the Chinese culture. In that case, we could find numerous cultural points of view and cultural elements being expressed through the language. This is a very interesting element of the Chinese language.

4. Sentence structures – Cause and Result

In Chinese grammar, there is a thing commonly used in the language called "Sentence Structures." It is **kind of a template** in which we can put the types of sentences (like "basic sentence" and "basic + time sentence" that we already have learned) on it. In illustration 3 below, you could see the template of a "cause and result" type of sentence.

Illustration 3: Sentence structure of cause and result

Basic sentence as learned in chapter 1

* Translation: Because I don't like the taste of coffee, therefore I don't drink coffee.

As you can see, the structure is as follows:

> Yīnwèi... , suǒyǐ...

This correlates with the meaning of:

> Because... , therefore...

5. The meaning of Zhōngguó ('China') in Chinese

China is composed of two words – **'middle'** + **'kingdom/country.'** What is the meaning of this? It means China saw itself since ancient times as the middle kingdom, as the ruler of East Asia, the main and central superpower in the region, an example and admiration model to other countries in social, technological, cultural etc.

This thing was actually true during Chinese history since the countries around China, such as Japan, Korea and more, adopted some of the Chinese language's cultural aspects and some of its writing systems still in use until today. These countries looked at China with admiration for its vast cultural, social and economic blooming.

Originally, in ancient times, the country created by Han people was called the lands of China as "Zhōngyuán," which means **"The central Chinese plains"** (which is today located at the Henan Province, in the Center-East part of China). It is important to say that China's Chinese name ("Zhōngguó") got its meaning only after the last Qing Empire, which reigned during 1644 – 1912.

6. Sentence order of adverbs yě, bù and dōu

There is an order for using the adverbs **'yě'**, **'bù'** and **'dōu.'**

* When you have yě in the sentence, it will be before 'bù' and 'dōu.'
** 'bù' can be before or after 'dōu' – depends on the meaning of the sentence.

Examples:

* Tāmén bù hē kāfēi.

(They [the boys] don't drink coffee)

** Tāmén yě dōu bù hē kāfēi.

(They [the girls] also <u>whole of them</u> don't drink coffee) =>

100% of them don't drink coffee.

** Tāmén yě bù dōu hē kāfēi.

(They [the girls] also <u>not everyone</u> drink coffee) =>

maybe 80% of them don't drink coffee.

7. Common phrases in Chinese

In Chinese language and any language, there are common-daily phrases that are part of modern talk. As we learn those phrases, it is important to keep in mind that sometimes there is no direct translation "as is" of the Chinese phrase to its parallel phrase in English. It is not always a direct translation. Therefore, these phrases **need to be memorized** and we need to be familiar with them to notice each time they are shown – in which context they are being said.

8. The neutral tone mark

The neutral tone mark represented by a dot '.' **is not always going to be shown** in the PinYin transcript system. Usually, it will be deducted. For example, instead of writing in PīnYīn as "wǒ .de," we will write "wǒ de."

9. Time and Place order in a sentence

As we mentioned before, in most cases, time will be <u>at the beginning of the sentence</u> in Chinese Grammar sentence structure. At the same time, <u>place specification will be added after the time</u> and not before it.

Formula:

> Time + Place + the rest of the sentence …

For example:

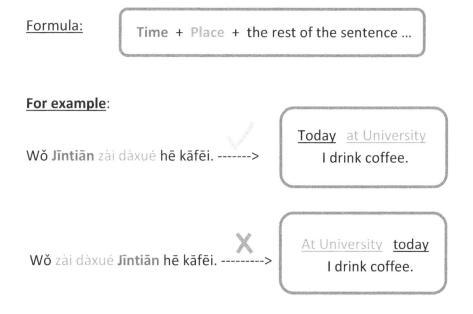

Wǒ **Jīntiān** zài dàxué hē kāfēi. ------->

> <u>Today</u> at University
> I drink coffee.

Wǒ zài dàxué **Jīntiān** hē kāfēi. --------->

> At University <u>today</u>
> I drink coffee.

10. The special verb 'zhù' (to live)

This verb is special because we will find this verb, differently than other verbs, **before the place and before zài** (in; at; inside).

For example: I live at Shànghǎi -----------------> wǒ zhù zài Shànghǎi.

I eat rice at Shànghǎi --------> wǒ zài Shànghǎi chī fàn.

11. The verb and preposition 'zài' (to be found at; at)

When 'zài' is in the sentence **with no other verbs**, it functions as a verb.
When **there is an additional verb** in the sentence except for 'zài,' it functions as a preposition.

For example:

wǒ **zài** cānguǎn. --------------------------> I **am (found) at** the restaurant.

wǒ **zài** cānguǎn hē chá. -----------> I am **at** the restaurant drinking tea.

12. The use of 'zài' as an auxiliary verb to express actions in progress

The verb 'zài' that we learned above, which could also be a preposition, has another nice use to describe an action in progress. It

50

is similar to the 'ing' in English, but here the 'ing' part ('Zài') comes **before** the verb and **not after it**.

The structure is:

Sub. + Zài + Verb + Obj.

For example**:** Tā zài xué Yīngwén. --------> which means: "He/She is learning English".

13. The use of 'Huì' in the phrase "Nǐ huì Zhōngwén ma?"

The literal meaning of the phrase **"Nǐ huì Zhōngwén ma?"** is **"Can you Chinese (language)?"**. There is no additional word here such as 'to talk' or 'to speak' so the sentence will literally say, "Can you speak Chinese (language)?", this is because this phrase is very common in Chinese language when asking people (and especially when Chinese are talking with foreigners) if they know how to speak some language (especially Chinese).

C. Exercises

Practicing the new vocabulary together with the new grammar points:

C.1. PīnYīn to English matching

Please match each word in English to its corresponding meaning in Chinese PīnYīn according to Chapter 3 vocabulary:

Xièxie	French
Shì	Work
Míng	Of
Fǎyǔ	Name
.De	Lawyer
Gōngzuò	Thank you
Lùshī	MW for honorable positions
Dàxué	To be called
Hǎo	English
Méi	Chinese language
Jiào	Rome
Zhù	China
Míngzì	To be (am; is; are)
Luómǎ	University
Zhōngguó	To live
Zhōngwén	In; At
Yīngwén	Past negation
Zài	Good

C.2. Sentence translation

According to this section's parts, please translate the following Chinese PinYin sentences into English and vice versa.

Note: Please pay special attention to the vocabulary and the sentence structures. In the first part of this exercise, it is recommended to read the sentences aloud before translating them into English to get familiar with the Mandarin Chinese tones which become a coherent part of your learning process. **In the second part**, it is recommended to read your translated work to see if it makes sense according to what we have learned so far.

* Ch ---> En (Chinese into English)

1. Nǐ zài Luómǎ chī fàn ma?

   _____

2. Wǒ zài Zhōngguó de dàxué xué Zhōngwén.

   _____

3. Tā zhù zài Fǎguó. Tā de gōngzuò shì lǜshī.

   _____

4. Nǐhǎo, nǐ gàn ma?

   _____

5. Wǒ bùcuò, xièxie nǐ.

   _____

6. Zhàoměi hé Máodì dōu zài Bālí gōngzuò.

   _____

7. Nǐhǎo! Nǐ zuìjìn zěnme yang? Hái kěyǐ ma?

_____

8. Hái kěyǐ, lǎo yàngzi.

_____

9. Tā méi chī fàn, shì bù hǎo.

_____

10. Nǐhǎo, wǒ jiào Dàwèi (David).

_____

11. Wǒ de míngzì shì Máodì.

_____

12. Nǐ shì Déguó rén háishi Fǎguó rén?

_____

13. Wǒ hé nǐ zài Bālí chī Fǎcān.

_____

14. Tā shì yī míng lǜshī.

_____

15. Tā yě shì yī míng lǜshī.

_____

16. Tāmén dōu shì hǎo lùshī.

_____

17. Nǐhǎo ma? Nǐ Jīntiān zài Luómǎ xué Yìdàlìyǔ ma? Bùcuò!

_____

18. Wǒ zài Yīngguó de gōngsī gōngzuò.

_____

19. nǐ de gōngzuò hǎo ma?

_____

20. Wǒmén yě dōu zài lùshī shìwùsuǒ gōngzuò.

_____

* En ---> Ch (English into Chinese)

1. I am in China, not in France.

_____

2. I learn Chinese.

_____

3. I am a Parisian.

_____

55

4. Do you live in Rome?

_____

5. I live in Germany. I work in a Lawyer's company.

_____

6. He is a student. He and she learn Chinese.

_____

7. They learn Italian and Chinese.

_____

8. How are you? Still ok?

_____

9. How is it recently?

_____

10. Same, all the same, thanks.

_____

11. I'm being called Richard.

_____

12. My name is Zhàoměi.

_____

13. I didn't drink coffee.

_____

14. Are you Chinese?

_____

15. Are you an Italian?

_____

16. Are you British?

_____

17. Are you French?

_____

18. He is at university studies English.

_____

19. I live in China.

_____

20. I live in France.

_____

21. He is a (honorable) lawyer.

_____

C.3. Text

Nǐhǎo, wǒ de míngzì shì Máodì, wǒ shì Zhōngguórén. Wǒ zài lǜshī shìwùsuǒ gōngzuò. Tā yě shì yī míng lǜshī. Wǒ hé tā dōu gōngzuò. Tā shì Yīngguórén, tā zhù zài Zhōngguó. Yīnwèi tā zài Zhōngguó gōngzuò, suǒyǐ tā zài xué Zhōngwén.

* Please try to translate the Text from Chinese PinYin into English:

_____

_____

_____

_____

_____

_____

D. Chapter summary

We just finished Chapter 3, and the next chapter, after our usual Culture Corner in this chapter, will be dedicated to sum it all up, starting from chapter 1 to chapter 3. Take a small break and continue with our journey.

E. The culture corner

Chinese Characters

The Chinese characters are very special since they combine sounds and symbols/drawings **all together**. The significance of the written language in Chinese is very deep since all the tradition transferred from one generation to another was all via the written media, and less by spoken language. In the year of 221 B.C., the emperor of Qin was the first ruler that united all types of written scripts into one standard and written script. In the next book, we will learn the Simplified Chinese Characters, and we will find out their beauty and meaning.

Illustration 4: The simplified writing of the words "Chinese language" in Chinese.

Zhōngwén

Answers for chapter 3

C.1. PīnYīn to English matching

Xièxie	French
Shì	Work
Míng	Of
Fǎyǔ	Name
.De	Lawyer
Gōngzuò	Thank you
Lǜshī	MW for honorable positions
Dàxué	To be called
Hǎo	English
Méi	Chinese language
Jiào	Rome
Zhù	China
Míngzì	To be (am; is; are)
Luómǎ	University
Zhōngguó	To live
Zhōngwén	In; At
Yīngwén	Past negation
Zài	Good

C.2. Sentence translation

* Ch ---> En (Chinese into English)

1. Are you in Rome eating rice?

2. I'm at a Chinese university learning Chinese language.

3. He lives in France. He works as a lawyer.

4. Hello, what are you up to?

5. I'm ok, thank you.

6. Zhaomei and Maodi (They) all work in Paris.

7. Hi! How are you recently? Still doing well?

8. Still fine, same same.

9. He didn't eat food, (it) is not good.

10. Hello, I'm being called David.

11. My name is Maodi.

12. Are you German? French?

13. You and I (are) in Paris eating French food.

14. He is a (honorable) lawyer.

15. He is also a (honorable) lawyer.

16. They are both good lawyers.

17. What's up? Are you in Rome today studying Italian? Not bad!

18. I work at a British company.

19. Is your work good?

20. We are also all working at Lawyers Company.

* En ---> Ch (English into Chinese)

1. wǒ zài Zhōngguó, bù zài Fǎguó.

2. Wǒ xué Zhōngwén.

3. Wǒ shì yī gè Bālí rén.

4. Nǐ zhù zài Luómǎ ma?

5. Wǒ zhù zài Déguó. Wǒ zài lǜshī shìwùsuǒ gōngzuò.

6. Tā shì yī gè xuéshēng. Tā hé tā (dōu) xué Zhōngwén.

7. Tāmén xué Yìdàlìyǔ hé Zhōngwén.

8. Nǐhǎo ma? Hái kěyǐ ma?

9. Nǐ zuìjìn zěnme yàng?

10. Lǎo yàngzi, xièxie.

11. Wǒ jiào Richard.

12. Wǒ de míngzì shì Zhàoměi.

13. Wǒ méi hē kāfēi.

14. Nǐ shì Zhōngguórén ma?

15. Nǐ shì Yìdàlì rén ma?

16. Nǐ shì Yīngguó rén ma?

17. Nǐ shì Fǎguó rén ma?

18. Tā zài dàxué xué Yīngwén.

19. Wǒ zhù zài Zhōngguó.

20. Wǒ zhù zài Fǎgúo.

21. Tā shì yī míng lǜshī.

C.3. Text

Hello, my name is Maodi. I am a Chinese person. I work at lawyer's company. He is also an honorable lawyer. He and I are both working. He is British, and he lives in China. Because he works in China, Therefore (he) is studying Chinese.

Revision on chapters 1 - 3

A. Vocabulary summary:

Times		Verbs	
Zǎoshàng	Early morning	Chī	To eat
Xiàwǔ	Afternoon	Hē	To drink
Wǎnshàng	evening		
Měitiān	Every day		
		Nouns	
		Kāfēi	Coffee
Pronouns		Shuǐ	Water
Wǒ	I; Me	Fàn	Food; Rice
Nǐ	You		
Tā	He; She; It	**Adverbs**	
		Bù	No
Question Words		**Conjunctions**	
.ma	Particle expressing a question	Hé	And

Times

Zhōngwǔ	Noon
.De shí.hou	While / When (doing something)
Yèlǐ	Night
jīntiān	Today

Pronouns

Wǒmén	We
Nǐmén	You (Plural)
Tāmén	They

Adverbs

Yě	Also (comes before a verb)
Dōu	All / Everyone / Everything / In all cases

Measure words

Wǎn	MW for bowls
Bēi	MW for cups
Shuāng	MW for pairs
Gè	General MW

Verbs

Gěi	To give
Diǎn	To order (a dish)
Qù	To go
Qǐng	To ask / to invite somebody to somewhere
Yào	To want / To need

Nouns

Cài	A dish
Kuàizi	Chopsticks
Mǐfàn	Cooked rice
Chá	Tea
Wǎn	Bowl
Tāng	Soup
Cānguǎn	Restaurant

Numbers

Yī	One
Èr	Two (ordinal number)
Sān	Three

Liǎng	Two (for counting)

Adjectives

Hǎo	Good
Bùcuò	Not bad

Common Phrases

nǐhǎo	Hello
nǐhǎo .ma?	How are you?
xièxie	Thank you
Zuìjìn zěnme yàng?	How Is it recently?
Hái kěyǐ	Still ok
Lǎo yàngzi	Same same
Nǐ gàn .ma?	What are you up to?

Verbs

Shì	To be (am/is/are)
Xué	To learn/To study
Zhù	To live
Gōngzuò	To work
Jiào	To be called
Zài	To be located at
Gàn	To do
Huì	Can (to know how to do something)

Nouns

Zhōngguó	China
Rén	A person; People
Rénmen	People (The public; Random people in the street)
Fǎguó	France
Déguó	Germany

Nouns

		Bālí	Paris
Zhàoměi	A girl called Zhaomei	Luómā	Rome
Máodì	A boy called Maodi	Xuéshēng	A student
		Dàxué	University
		Gōngzuò	Work
Adverbs		Lǜshī	Lawyer
		Shìwùsuǒ	Business office
Méi	Past negation	gōngsī	Company
Háishi	Still; Or (in question form)	Fǎcān	French dish/food
Zhèngzài	Right now form (-ing)	Wèidào	Taste
		Míngzì	Name
		Yīngwén	English language
		Zhōngwén	Chinese language
Possessions		Fǎyǔ	French language
.De	Of (possession particle)	Yìdàlìyǔ	Italian language
Wǒ de	Mine		
Nǐ de	Yours	Measure Words	
Tā de	His/Hers/Its		
		Míng	MW for honorable

			positions (lawyers, doctors, etc.)
Prepositions		Auxiliary Verbs	
Zài	At; In; On		
		Zài	Expressing actions in progress (-ing)

B. Grammar points summary:

1. Basic sentence structure

> Subject + (Adverb) + Verb + Object

2. Basic sentence + time structure

> **Time** + Subject + (Adverb) + Verb + Object

3. Time order:

> Year + Month + Day

4. Measure words:

Separating nouns and characteristics of processes in nature into different categories such as round things, flat things, things with handle, things that look like a stick, etc.

5. The Counting Formula:

> Number + Measure Word + Noun

6. Chinese names

- Family name is before the given name.
- Great deal of respect for someone's name.
- Adopting a western name by young people nowadays in China, according to Confucius philosophy, which suggests that a person's name must match and should correspond with its current character, manners and state of mind.

7. Possession

- De = of (something / someone)
- Wǒ de ---> Mine, Nǐ de -----> yours.

8. The word 'wén' and its different meanings

- Wén = language; culture

- Language is a means that reflects the cultural view of Chinese people about reality, themselves and the world.

9. Sentence structures – Cause and result

- Sentence structures are common in Chinese language.
- The common structures are sort of a "template" which we Place the regular sentences on it.
- The structure is: **"Because** (yīnwèi)..., **therefore** (suǒyǐ)...".

10. The meaning of Zhōngguó ('China') in Chinese

- The word China is composed of two words – 'Middle' + 'Kingdom/Country'.
- Originally, in ancient times, the country created by Han people was called the lands of China as 'Zhōngyuán', which means **"The central Chinese plains,"** located at today's Henan Province.

11. Sentence order of adverbs yě, bù and dōu

- when you have yě in the sentence, it will be **before** bù and dōu.
- bù can be before or after dōu – depending on the meaning of the sentence.

- **Ex**: Tāmén yě dōu bù **/** bù dōu hē kāfēi.

12. Common phrases in Chinese

- Common phrases in Chinese language are not always translated directly to English; memorization and adaptation are necessary in most cases.

13. The neutral tone mark

- The neutral tone mark represented by a dot '.' is not always going to be shown.
- Ex: wǒ .de = wǒ de

14. Time and place order in a sentence

- Time at the beginning of the sentence
- Place **after** the time in the sentence
- Formula: **Time** + **Place** + the rest of the sentence...

15. the special verb 'zhù' (to live)

- We will find this verb differently than other verbs, **before the place and before zài**.
- a. wǒ zhù zài Shànghǎi.   b. wǒ zài Shànghǎi **chī** fàn.

16. The verb and preposition 'zài' (to be found at; at)

- When 'zài' is in the sentence **with no other verbs**, it functions as a **verb**.
- When **there is an additional verb** in the sentence except for 'zài,' it functions as a **preposition**.

17. The use of 'zài' as an auxiliary verb to express actions in progress

Sub. + Zài + Verb + Obj.

18. The use of 'Huì' in the phrase "Nǐ huì Zhōngwén ma?"

The literal meaning of the phrase "Nǐ huì Zhōngwén ma?" is "Can you Chinese (language)?".

There is no additional word here such as 'to talk' or 'to speak' so the sentence will literally say, "Can you speak Chinese (language)?", this is because this phrase is very common in Chinese language when asking people (and especially when Chinese are talking with foreigners) if they know how to speak some language (especially Chinese).

C. Exercises

C.1. Translation sentences Practice (makes perfect!) – chapters 1-3

* Ch -------> En Translation

1. Wǒ qù cānguǎn.

_____

2. Nǐ qù cānguǎn ma?

_____

3. Tā yě qù cānguǎn ma?

_____

4. Wǒmén dōu qù cānguǎn.

_____

5. Tāmén yě dōu qù cānguǎn.

_____

6. Wǒ yào diǎn cài.

_____

7. Nǐ yào diǎn cài ma?

_____

8. Tā yě yào diǎn cài ma?

_____

9. Tā bù yào diǎn cài.

_____

10. Qǐng gěi wǒ chá.

_____

11. Qǐng gěi wǒ liǎng bēi chá.

_____

12. Tāmén yào diǎn sān wǎn mǐfàn.

_____

13. Wǒmén yě yào diǎn sān wǎn mǐfàn.

_____

14. Qǐng gěi wǒ yī wǎn tāng.

_____

15. Wǒ yào hē shuǐ, nǐ yě yào ma?

_____

16. Tā yào hē kāfēi, nǐ yě yào ma?

_____

17. Nǐ shì Zhōngguórén ma?

_____

18. Tā shì Yīngguórén ma?

_____

19. Yīnwèi wǒ bù shì Zhōngguórén, suǒyǐ wǒ yào xué Zhōngwén.

_____

20. Yīnwèi wǒ yào chī fàn, suǒyǐ wǒ diǎn yī wǎn tāng hé yǐ wǎn
    mǐfàn.

_____

_____

21. Nǐ zhù zài Zhōngguó ma?

_____

22. Wǒ bù zhù zài Yīngguó.

_____

23. Tāmén bù dōu shì Yīngguórén.

_____

24. Wǒ zài gōngsī gōngzuò.

_____

25. Tā yě zài gōngsī gōngzuò.

_____

26. Wǒ zài lǜshī shìwùsuǒ gōngzuò.

_____

27. Wǒ zài Zhōngguó lǜshī shìwùsuǒ gōngzuò.

_____

28. Wǒ jiào Dàwèi (David).

_____

29. Tā jiào Zhàoměi.

_____

30. Tā de míngzì shì Máodì.

_____

31. Yīnwèi wǒmén dōu zài gōngsī gōngzuò, suǒyǐ yào qù cānguǎn chī fàn.

_____

_____

32. Zhōngwǔ de shíhou wǒmén qù cānguǎn.

_____

33. Měitiān wǎnshàng wǒ hē kāfēi.

_____

34. Tā zhù zài Bālí.

_____

35. Wǒ yě zhù zài Bālí.

_____

36. Nǐ zhù zài Bālí ma?

_____

37. Qǐng gěi wǒ yī shuāng kuàizi.

_____

38. Nǐ huì Fǎyǔ ma?

_____

39. Wǒ méi hē chá.

_____

40. Tā yě méi hē chá.

_____

* EN -------> Ch Translation

1. In the (time of the) morning, I drink tea.

_____

2. Would you like tea?

_____

3. Please give us three cups of coffee.

_____

4. I learn Chinese and Italian.

   _____

5. I invite you to drink coffee.

   _____

6. I live in France, Paris.

   _____

7. I am at the restaurant.

   _____

8. Because I am not a student, therefore I am not in university.

   _____

9. We all work at Lawyer's company.

   _____

10. My name is Oscar.

   _____

11. I am being called Maria.

   _____

12. Please give me one bowl of soup and two bowls of cooked rice.

_____

_____

13. I am at the restaurant drinking tea.

_____

14. Are they also at the restaurant?

_____

15. I don't want chopsticks. Thanks.

_____

16. Are you a student?

_____

17. How are you recently?

_____

18. Same same, thank you.

_____

19. Hello! What are you up to?

_____

20. He is a (honorable) lawyer.

_____

21. We also at the company.

_____

22. I live in Paris. Do you live in Rome?

_____

23. We all live in China.

_____

24. Today, in the morning, I didn't eat (food).

_____

25. Do you learn Italian?

_____

26. Do you and he live in China?

_____

27. At night time, I don't drink coffee.

_____

28. Today, in the afternoon, I didn't eat rice.

_____

29. Please give me 2 cups of water.

_____

30. Do you also want water?

_____

31. I drink tea, thank you.

_____

32. Are you German?

_____

33. Are you Chinese?

_____

34. Are you French?

_____

35. Are you Italian?

_____

36. Because I live in France, therefore I learn French.

_____

37. Because I want to drink tea; therefore, you and I will go to the restaurant to drink tea.

_____

38. Every day in the morning, I eat rice.

_____

39. I live in England.

_____

40. I drink water, he drinks tea, and you drink coffee.

_____

C.2. Text

Zhàoměi: Nǐhǎo, nǐ zuìjìn zěnme yàng?

Máodì: Hái kěyǐ.

Zhàoměi: Nǐ zài gōngzuò ma?

Máodì: Shì, wǒ zài gōngsī gōngzuò. Nǐ Jīntiān gànmá le?

Zhàoměi: Wǒ Jīntiān zǎoshàng xué le Zhōngwén. Xiàwù de shíhòu wǒ yě xué le Zhōngwén.

Máodì: Bùcuò, bùcuò.

Zhàoměi: Xièxie Máodi. Nǐ yào qù cānguǎn chī fàn ma? Wǒ méi chī **wǎnfàn** (dinner).

Máodì: **Hǎo. Wǒ yào hē tāng hé chī mǐfàn.**

C.3. Please answer questions 1-3 in **PīnYīn** and answer question 4 in **English**:

1. Where was Maodi during his conversation with Zhaomei?

_____

2. Did Zhaomei eat dinner or not?

_____

3. Is Zhaomei a good student? If yes, Please copy the sentence that says so.

_____

4. Please translate to English the **bold lined sentence** in the dialogue:

_____

Answers for revision on chapters 1 - 3

C.1. Translation sentences Practice (makes perfect!) – chapters 1-3:

* Ch -------> En Translation

1. I went to a restaurant.
2. Did you go to a restaurant?
3. Did he also go to a restaurant?
4. We all went to a restaurant.
5. They also all went to a restaurant.
6. I want to order a dish.
7. Would you like to order a dish?
8. Does he also want to order a dish?
9. She doesn't want to order a dish.

10. Please give me tea.

11. Please give me two cups of tea.

12. They want to order three bowls of rice.

13. We also want to order three bowls of rice.

14. Please give me one bowl of soup.

15. I would like to drink water, do you also want?

16. He wants to drink coffee, do you also want?

17. Are you Chinese?

18. Is he British?

19. Because I'm not a Chinese (person); therefore, I would like to learn Chinese language.

20. Because I want to eat food; therefore, I ordered one bowl of soup and one bowl of cooked rice.

21. Do you live in China?

22. I don't live in England.

23. Not all of them are British.

24. I am at the company working.

25. He is also at the company working.

26. I am at lawyer's company working.

27. I am at a Chinese lawyer's company working.

28. I am called David.

29. She is called Zhaomei.

30. His name is Maodi.

31. Because we are all at the company working, therefore we want to go to a restaurant to eat (some food).

32. At noon, we will go to the restaurant.

33. Every day in the evening, I drink coffee.

34. He lives in Paris.

35. I also live in Paris.

36. Do you live in Paris?

37. Please give me one pair of chopsticks.

38. Do you learn French?

39. I do not drink tea.

40. He/She also do not drink tea.

* EN -------> Ch Translation

1. Zǎoshàng de shíhou wǒ hē chá.

2. Nǐ yào chá ma?

3. Qǐng gěi wǒmén sān bēi kāfēi.

4. Wǒ xué Zhōngwén hé Yìdàlìyǔ.

5. Wǒ qǐng nǐ hē kāfēi.

6. Wǒ zhù zài Fǎguó, Bālí.

7. Wǒ zài cānguǎn.

8. Yīnwèi wǒ bùshì yī gè xuéshēng, suǒyǐ wǒ bù zài dàxué.

9. Wǒmén dōu zài lǜshī de gōngsī gōngzuò.

10. Wǒ de míngzì shì Oscar.

11. Wǒ jiào Maria.

12. Qǐng gěi wǒ yī wǎn tāng hé liǎng wǎn mǐfàn.

13. Wǒ zài cānguǎn hē chá.

14. Tāmén yě zài cānguǎn ma?

15. Wǒ bù yào kuàizi, xièxie.

16. Nǐ shì yī gè xuéshēng ma?

17. Nǐ zuìjìn zěnme yàng?

18. Lǎo yàngzi, xièxie.

19. Nǐhǎo! Nǐ gàn me?

20. Tā shì yī míng lǜshī.

21. Wǒmén yě zài gōngsī.

22. Wǒ zhù zài Bālí. Nǐ zhù zài Luómā ma?

23. Wǒmén dōu zhù zài Zhōngguó.

24. Jīntiān zǎoshàng wǒ méi chī fàn.

25. Nǐ xué Yìdàlìyǔ ma?

26. Nǐ hé tā zhù zài Zhōngguó ma?

27. Yèlǐ de shíhou wǒ bù hē kāfēi.

28. Jīntiān Xiàwǔ wǒ méi chī fàn.

29. Qǐng gěi wǒ liǎng bēi shuǐ.

30. Nǐ yě yào shuǐ ma?

31. Wǒ hē chá, xièxie.

32. Nǐ shì Déguó rén ma?

33. Nǐ shì Zhōngguórén ma?

34. Nǐ shì Fǎguó rén ma?

35. Nǐ shì Yìdàlì rén ma?

36. Yīnwèi wǒ zhù zài Fǎguó, suǒyǐ wǒ xué Fǎyǔ.

37. Yīnwèi wǒ yào hē chá, suǒyǐ wǒ hé nǐ dōu qù cānguǎn hē chá.

38. Měitiān zǎoshàng wǒ chī fàn.

39. Wǒ zhù zài Yīngguó.

40. Wǒ hē shuǐ, tā hē chá, nǐ hē kāfēi

C.3. Answering questions 1 – 4 about the text:

1. Máodì zài gōngsī.
2. Zhàoměi méi chī wǎnfàn.
3. "Wǒ Jīntiān zǎoshàng xué le Zhōngwén. Xiàwù de shíhòu wǒ yě xué le Zhōngwén."
4. "Good/OK. I want to drink soup and eat cooked rice."

* Before we continue to the next Chapter...

As I mentioned at the start of this book, in the "**Tones – Explanation and practice**" section, we have 3 tone rules that show us how to manage a Mandarin Chinese conversation. Please look at table 4 for the following three common tone rules:

Table 4: Most Basic Tone Rules

Tone rule	Explanation	Example
3rd tone + 3rd tone ---> 2nd tone + 3nd tone	When we have <u>two</u> <u>3rd tones in a row</u>, we will read the first 3rd tone as <u>a</u> <u>2nd tone</u>.	Wǒ yě yào hē shuǐ. ---> Wó yě yào hē shuǐ.

bù + 4th tone ---> bú + 4th tone	When we have the 4th tone after the word 'no' in Chinese ('**bù**'), we should read the word as 'bú' – with the 2nd tone.	Tā bù yào hē kāfēi. ---> Tā bú yào hē kāfēi.
* yī + 4th tone ---> yí + 4th tone * yī + 1st/2nd/3rd tone ---> yì + 1st/2nd/3rd tone	* When we have the word 'one,' which is 'yī' (in the first tone), the tone will change to 2nd tone if a 4th tone comes after the word. * For **any other tone** that comes after 'yī' (**1st /2nd or 3rd tone**), it will be changed to 4th tone.	* Tā shì yī gè rén. ---> Tā shì yí gè rén. * Yī wǎn tāng. ---> Yì wǎn tāng.

As we can see in the table, 3 main rules guide the addition of tones **while reading words in a sentence flow.**

Chapter 4

How Do I Arrive at The Movies?

A. Vocabulary

Verbs		Times	
Zǒu	To step to; To walk to	Yǐhòu	After
Guǎi	To turn to	Yǐqián	Before
Zhuǎn	To turn to	Zhīhòu	Right after (an action)
Yǒu	To have	Zhīqián	Right before (an action)
Xiǎng	To think (about doing something); To miss (someone)		

Nouns		Daily phrases	
Lǐ	Inside		
		Qǐngwèn	Excuse me...; I would like to ask, please...
Bīnguǎn	Hotel		
Lù	Way		
Kǒu	Mouth	Jiùshì	Simply is...; Really is...
		Jiùzài	Is just at...

Nouns

Colors

Yánsè	Color

Lùkǒu	Intersection
Jiā	Home; Family
Dēng	Light
Jiē	Street
Hónglǜdēng	Traffic light
Diàn	Electricity
Yǐng	Shadow
Diànyǐng	Movie
Yuàn	Courtyard
Diànyǐngyuàn	Cinema
Yínháng	Bank

Hóngsè	Red
Lǜsè	Green
Hēisè	Black
Huángsè	Yellow
Lánsè	Blue
Fěnsè	Pink
Huīsè	Grey
Zǐsè	Purple
Chéngsè	Orange

Adverbs

Jiù	Then; Just
Děi	Must to; Have to
Hái	Still

Directions

Yòu	Right
Zuǒ	Left
Yīzhí	Straight
Biān	Side
Duìmiàn	In front of

Prepositions

Lǐ	In
Wǎng	To (somewhere)

Question words

Zěnme?	How?; How to?
Nǎr? / Nǎ lǐ?	Where?

Measure words		Auxiliary words	
Jiā	MW for Buildings and businesses	Dì	Auxiliary word for ordinal numbers (**the** first, **the** second, **the** third...)

Numbers

Sì	Four
Wǔ	Five
Liù	Six
Qī	Seven
Bā	Eight
Jiǔ	Nine
Shí	Ten
Shíyī	Eleven
Shíèr	Twelve
Shísān	Thirteen
Èrshí	Twenty
Yībǎi	One hundred

Note: This vocabulary is of **directions and navigation** in the streets of China. When you walk down the streets of cities in China to get directions to the nearest train station, Metro station, bank, local restaurant, or the nearest Starbucks, you would definitely be assisted by this chapter with its vocabulary and phrases.

B. Grammar

1. The expression "Qǐngwèn."

This expression means "excuse me please..." It is useful for western tourists who would like to ask some questions while in China's public places such as streets, at the supermarket, at the ticket counter, near a subway, etc. This expression will be shown first and after it, we will place the relevant question that we would like someone to assist us with.

Structure: * "Qǐngwèn, ...?"

Example: * "Qǐngwèn, dìtiě zěnme zǒu?"

(Meaning: "Excuse me please, how do I go to the subway?")

2. WH Questions

The WH questions are, "Where?" "When?" "How?" "How much?" "Why?" "What?" "Who?", "Which?", etc. In these types of questions, we are requesting an answer to a reason, purpose, specific time, specific place and more.

In Chinese language, when you ask a question with WH Questions, the answer to the question will usually and **in most cases replace the WH Question itself**. In the answer, we just need to change the pronoun ('you' ---> 'I') and put the answer instead of the WH question.

Ex: <u>WH Question:</u> "nǐ zài nǎr?"   ------------>   "where are you at?"

<u>Answer:</u> "wǒ zài jiā."   -------------------->   "I am at home."

3. Counting objects with " Dì"

Counting objects in Chinese is made by the ordinal particle "Dì," which means "the first," "the second," "the third," and so on. With this counting particle, we need to remember to use the word "Èr" for "the 2nd (item)" in Chinese, and not with the word "Liǎng," as with the first numbers we learned in chapter 3.

<u>Structure:</u>

Dì + number

4. Changing Direction formula

So here we are, we arrived at the part of directions in our learning process. When we would like to hang out with our friends or travel in China city streets, we would like to ask for directions on how to go to the nearest bank, nearest subway station, movies, book store, pharmacy store, supermarket, attraction site and many more, so we could use this nice formula.

The formula contains **3 parts** -----> 'towards' + side + '(to) turn'

Let's see an example: Ch: "wǎng   yòu   guǎi."

                            En: "towards   right (side)   turn."

And let's summarize it:

> Wǎng + zuǒ / yòu + zhuǎn / guǎi

5. The expression "How to go to (somewhere)?" -------> "Zěnme zǒu?"

The question "how to go to (somewhere)?" is expressed in Chinese as "zěnme zǒu?". It acctually means "how to (get somewhere by) walk to?". It is also used only at the end of the sentence after the location you want to go to.

Structure:

> Location + zěnme zǒu?

For example: * Dìtiě (Subway) zěnme zǒu?

                    * Gōngyuán (Park) zěnme zǒu?

** Pay attention to use **'zǒu'** and not 'qù', which also means 'to go'.

C. Exercises

Practicing vocabulary with grammar:

C.1. Text completion

Please complete the following sentences with the right word from the brackets:

Zhàoměi: Nǐhǎo, Máodì. Wǒ qǐng_____(nǐ / wǒ) qù cānguǎn

hē_____(tāng / fàn).

Máodì: Hǎo, cānguǎn zěnme_____(zǒu / qù)?

Zhàoměi: Wǒmen (yī / èr) zhí zǒu, dì sān (gè / wǎn) lùkǒu yòu zhuǎn,

zhīhòu, yīzhí zǒu, diànyǐngyuàn jiù (yǒu / zài) wǒmen de zuǒbiān.

Diànyǐngyuàn duìmiàn jiùshì yī_____ (jiā / gè) cānguǎn.

Máodì: Zài cānguǎn wǒ yào_____(gěi / diǎn) liǎng wǎn

mǐ____(chī / fàn) hé yī____(gè / bēi) hóngchá.

Zhàoměi: Wǒ yě yào diǎn yī bēi hóngchá. Yīnwèi wǒmen shì

Zhōngguó rén, suǒyǐ wǒmen yě yào____(hē / chī) lǜchá.

C.2. Sentence translation

Please translate the following sentences into English:

1. Qǐngwèn, yínháng zěnme zǒu?

_____

2. Nǐ yào yīzhí zǒu, dì èr gè lùkǒu wǎng zuǒ guǎi, zhīhòu yīzhí zǒu. Dì
èr gè hónglǜdēng yòu zhuǎn. Cānguǎn jiùzài nǐ de yòubiān. Cānguǎn
duìmiàn jiùshì yī jiā yínháng.

_____

_____

_____

_____

_____

C.3. Guiding Zhàoměi to the restaurant

In the following illustration, you can see a street segment where **you
are requested to assist Zhàoměi to arrive at the Restaurant**. You
can assist by the previous section (C.2.2.).

Illustration 3: Example of China street segment

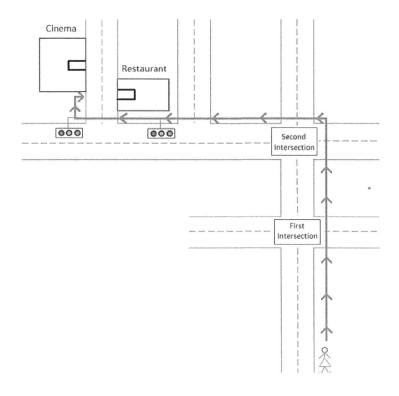

_____

_____

_____

_____

_____

D. Chapter summary

So, in this chapter, we covered the issue of the directions. We also talked about colors, learned new formulas and continued on numbers. In the next chapter, we will talk about weather and traveling in general, and we will talk about China's amazing attraction sites, particularly ^_^

E. The culture corner

Rice and Noodles in China

About 5,000 years ago, ancient Chinese people started growing and cultivating rice. Since the lands in China around the Yellow River and the Yangtze River is quite fertile and suitable for raising this kind of crop until now, and the population around these rivers was so immense, rice was exactly suitable as a basic food of China. Since ancient times, rice is considered the "bread of East Asian cultures", so this concept is still in China. Westerners worldwide can see that rice is basic food. Other complementary food (such as meat and vegetables) is being served or mixed in all kinds of cooking methods.

The growing of rice is done in water-flooded fields, while the fields are usually located on a plain surface or top of a mountain terrace. Each Chinese family in the country area has its own lot and they meticulously raise their rice there.

The rice planting is being made in a precise and tediously way, in which the Chinese people are expert in. They do this process while repeatedly bending for each planting square, while their legs are in the water and mud, and insects are occasionally around. The Chinese have a lot of patience for these kinds of processes, making them one of the most admirable diligent working forces in the world. The planting process probably gave the Chinese strength and flexibility to endure long hours of working in conditions the western man, in many cases, are not used to.

Noodle is an interesting story by itself. There is no much water in some regions in China, and the climate is dry and not humid. Therefore, rice is not the proper crop to grow in this kind of environment; therefore, another crop is necessary. Contrary to China's southern regions, the **northern** regions are characterized by a dry and cold climate. This kind of climate is perfect for millet and wheat crops that don't need too much water for their growth. So wheat became more common in these regions, which led to the making of the famous noodles.

Like rice, noodles are also a great basic substance that can be combined with multiple meat types, vegetables, spices, etc. Chinese people have many ways to cook their favorite noodles. Since the first noodle was made years ago, this has made them known as experts worldwide in the field of noodles making, cooking and serving.

Picture 5:
Croissant is being named in a local Chinese supermarket as "Western Bread". This culture point is very interesting because we can see how Chinese people look at products imported from the west, in this case from France.

Answers for chapter 4

C.1. Text completion

- Nǐ
- Tāng

- Zǒu
- Yī
- Gè
- Zài
- Jiā
- Diǎn
- Fàn
- Bēi
- Hē

C.2. Sentence translation

1. Excuse me, How do I go to the Bank?

2. You need to go straight, at the second intersection towards the left, turn right and then go straight. At the second traffic light, turn right. The restaurant is just on your right side. In front of the restaurant, there is a bank.

.3. Guiding Zhàoměi to the Restaurant

- **One possible option** for an answer is as followed:

Yī zhí zǒu. Dì èr gè lùkǒu <u>wǎng zuǒ guǎi</u> / <u>zuǒ zhuǎn</u>, zhīhòu yī zhí zǒu. Dì èr gè hónglǜdēng <u>wǎng yòu guǎi</u> / <u>yòu zhuǎn</u>. Diànyǐngyuàn jiùzài nǐ de duìmiàn. Diànyǐngyuàn duìmiàn jiùshì yī jiā cānguǎn.

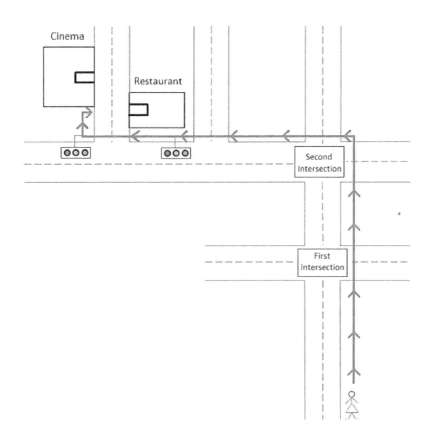

Chapter 5

Traveling in China

A. Vocabulary

Times		Nouns	
Zuótiān	Yesterday	Yīfú	Cloths
Míngtiān	Tomorrow	Dàyī	Overcoat
Nián	Year	Wàzi	Sock
Qùnián	Last year	Wéijīn	Scarf
Míngnián	Next year	Xínglǐ	Luggage
Xīngqi / Lǐbài	Week	Màozi	Hat
Yuè	Month	Chènshān	Shirt
Xiàtiān	Summer	Kùzi	Pants
Qiūtiān	Autumn	Huā	Flower
Dōngtiān	Winter	Shù	Tree
Chūntiān	Spring	Tàiyáng	Sun
		Yǔ	Rain
		Xuě	Snow
		Fēng	Wing

Pronouns			
Zhè; Zhèi (gè)	This / This one	Verbs	
Nà; Nèi (gè)	That / That one		
		Hěn	To be (comes before an adjective)

Adjectives			
Xíng	Okay	Dài	To take; To carry
Lěng	Cold	Mǎi	To buy
		Chuān	To wear
Rè	Hot	Dài	To put on

Nuǎn	Warm	Bāng (máng)	To help (with someone's matters)
Yīntiān	Cloudy day	Xūyào	Must; Have to; Need to
Qíngtiān	Sunny day	Dào	To arrive to; To go to
Qiángliè	Intense		

Question words

Adverbs

		Shénme?	What?; Which?
Hěn	Very	Wèi shénme?	Why?
Tài	Too much	Shénme shíhou?	When?
Zhēn	Really; Truly		

Measure words

Prepositions

Jiàn	MW for upper wear	Cóng	From
Tiáo	MW for pants		
Dǐng	MW for hats		

Sentence particles	
Le	Particle of status complement; Past tense particle

B. Grammar

1. The pronouns zhè; zhèi and nà; nèi

The meaning of the word 'zhè' is 'this,' and the meaning of the word 'zhèi' is 'this one.' The meaning of the word 'nà' is 'that,' and the meaning of the word 'nèi' is 'that one.' Instead of saying "zhè yī (gè) rén" for example (<u>means</u>: "this one person"), we can say "zhèi gè rén." This short use of pronouns is common and we occasionally use it as zhèi and nèi.

2. The use of 'hěn' with adjectives as the verb 'to be'

When we use the adverb 'hěn' in a simple sentence with an adjective, we use it like the verb **"to be"** (am; is; are). The meaning of **'hěn'** is 'very,' and it is used in more advanced sentences to show the degree of the adjective.

106

Example:

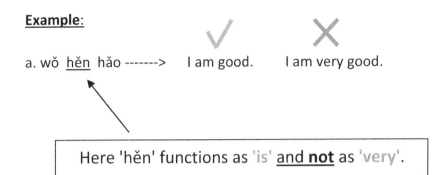

a. wǒ <u>hěn</u> hǎo -------> I am good.   I am very good.

Here 'hěn' functions as 'is' <u>**and not**</u> as 'very'.

3. The Predicate-Adjective type of sentence

We have learned different types of sentences, such as **basic sentences** and **basic sentences with time**. The next structure of the sentence we will learn is called the **Predicate-Adjective** sentence.

This kind of sentence is called that way since usually, the **predicate** of a regular sentence is most often a verb, but this kind of sentence is when the predicate is an **adjective**. So, in this kind of sentence, there will be no verb but an **adverb**.

Let's see the formula and some examples of this kind of sentence:

Subject + Adverb + Adjective

Examples:

<u>a</u>. Nǐ tài gāo. ----------------------> Tā (sub.) + tài (adv.) + gāo (adj.)

He (is)   too   tall.

<u>b</u>. Wǒ zhēn gāoxìng. ------> wǒ (sub.) + zhēn (adv.) + gāoxìng (adj.)

I (am)   really/truly   happy.

4. The phrase "Please help me with my business/issues" ----
-------> "Qǐng bāng wǒ de máng."

"Qǐng bang wǒ de máng" is a phrase that is built from Verb+Object
kind of verb,
or in short --------> VO.

bāng = to help   **máng = favor**

There is a lot of VO in Chinese, for example:

- chī fàn (to eat food).
- dú shū ("to read a book" – dú is like the word 'kàn').
- kāi chē (to drive a car).

The characteristic of these types of verbs is that they are separable.
Specifically, in "Bāngmáng," we can put "wǒ de" <u>before the object</u> to
make the object associate with someone.

<u>Ex:</u> "Qǐng bāng **wǒ de** máng." (= "Qǐng bāngmáng **wǒ**.")

5. Past tense le; New situation le

In Chinese grammar, one of the most important particles is the 'le' particle. This 'le' helps us to define the sentence time as past tense.

In addition, the **'le' particle** can also tell us if some action was completed or if there was any change in the action's state. Therefore, we call this kind of 'le' a "New situation le", which means that some reality has been changed and by adding 'le,' **the change is being declared**.

Pay attention: In this case of "New situation le", the 'le' particle in most cases will come at the end of the sentence, while at the "Past tense le", the 'le' particle will come right after the verb.

- "Past tense le" Structure:

> Subject + verb + le + (object).

- "New situation le" Structure:

> Subject + verb/Adj. .... + le.

Examples:

1. "Past tense le"

<u>a</u>. Tā mǎi le yī tiáo kùzi. ------------------> He bought one pair of pants.

<u>b</u>. Wǒmén chī le fàn. ------------------------------------> We ate food.

<u>c</u>. Tā chuān le yī jiàn chènshān. ------------------> He/She wear a shirt.

- In the case of <u>"past tense le"</u>, 'le' will often come **after the verb**, as we mentioned above.

2. "New situation le"

<u>a</u>. Wǒ chī wán le. ---> I finished eating.

(I was in a state of eating and finished eating).

<u>b</u>. Tā chī bǎo le. ----------------------------> He ate to his heart's content.

(He was eating and now he is totally full).

<u>c</u>. Tā è le. ---> He became hungry.

(He was ok and just now, he became hungry)

- In this case of <u>"New situation le"</u>, 'le' will often come **at the end of the sentence**, as we mentioned above.

C. Exercises

Practicing vocabulary with grammar:

C.1. Sentence translation (En -----> Ch)

1. In springtime in Beijing, there are red flowers and green trees.

   _____

2. Inside the luggage, there are socks, shirts, pants, one scarf and a hat.

   _____

3. Today is a cloudy day; the sun is not very intense.

   _____

4. I would like to buy one pair of red socks. He would like to buy one pair of blue socks.

   _____

   _____

5. What is this? Is it a coat?

   _____

6. It is winter now. Why don't you wear a coat?

_____

7. Can you help me with my stuff, please?

_____

8. Can I buy this scarf?

_____

C.2. Text translation and questions about the text

Zhàoměi: Zhè shì shénme?

Máodì: Zhè shì yī jiàn dàyī.

Zhàoměi: Zhè shì shénme?

Máodì: Zhè shì yī tiáo kùzi.

Zhàoměi: Nǐ qù Zhōngguó ma?

Máodì: Shì. Yīnwèi xiànzài zài Zhōngguó shì dōngtiān, suǒyǐ wǒ dài

dōngtiān de yīfú.

Zhàoměi: Dōngtiān de shíhòu, Zhōngguó hěn lěng mǎ?

Máodì: Dōngtiān de shíhòu, Zài Běijīng hěn lěng. Fēng, yǔ, xuě dōu yǒu. Wǒ xūyào dài yī gè wéijīn hé yī shuāng rè wàzi. Wǒ yě xūyào mǎi

yí xiāng xínglǐxiāng.

Zhàoměi: Nǐ shénme shíhòu qù Zhōngguó?

Máodì: Wǒ míngtiān qù Zhōngguó.

Zhàoměi: Nǐ yào wǒ bāng nǐ de máng ma?

Máodì: Nǐ wèishénme yào bāng wǒ?

Zhàoměi: Yīnwèi nǐ shì wǒ de péngyǒu, suǒyǐ wǒ yào bāng nǐ ya!

Máodì: Nǐ jiùshì hěn hǎo de péngyǒu.

Zhàoměi: Nǎlǐ nǎlǐ.

C.2.a. Text translation to English:

_____

_____

_____

_____

_____

_____

_____

_____

_____

_____

_____

_____

C.2.b. Questions about the text:

Please answer the following questions in Chinese:

1. Shéi míngtiān qù Zhōngguó?

   _____

2. Máodì zài xínglǐxiāng lǐ fàng le shénme ne?

   _____

   _____

   _____

   _____

_____

_____

_____

3. Zhàoměi wèishénme yào bāng Máodì?

_____

_____

_____

D. Chapter summary

This chapter was successfully finished! In your free time, please go to chapter 6 after having a small coffee and a cake break or a Chinese tea and a tea cookie, whatever you like. See you soon!

E. The culture corner

Cloisonné in China

Cloisonné is an art developed in China since the 13th century, for decorating copper items with colorful enamel filling. The technique was developed in ancient times and was made especially for jewelries, small artifacts and clothes. The copper items are being filled with all kinds of colors diligently and meticulously by artists. After being warmed to a high temperature, a beautiful piece of art can be seen.

This is only one of the examples of traditional art that came to China and which was developed locally, receiving its local style and character, a beautiful art thriving until today. Art and tradition are very important in China since a nation with a vast, diverse culture and legacy of customs and traditions are all contribute to a unified and a prosperous nation.

Picture 6: A Chinese woman in a Cloisonné factory in south China. The woman is stamping the copper and designing the shapes of the Cloisonné art on the copper vase, before filling it with colorful enamel.

Picture 7: A set of plates and vases from the Cloisonné art, shown as a finished product in the factory. The colorful items attract many Chinese and western tourists to see and buy it as wonderful decoration items for home or for office use.

Answers for chapter 5

C.1. Sentence translation (En -----> Ch)

1. Chūntiān zài Běijīng yǒu hóngsè de huā hé lǜsè de shù.
2. Zài xínglǐxiāng lǐ yǒu wàzi, chènshān, kùzi, yī tiáo wéijīn hé yī dǐng màozi.
3. Jīntiān shì yīntiān, tàiyáng bù tài qiángliè.
4. Wǒ yào mǎi yī shuāng hóngsè de wàzi. Tā yào mǎi yī shuāng lánsè de wàzi.
5. Zhè shì shénme? Zhè shì yī jiàn wàitào ma?
6. Xiànzài shì dōngtiān, nǐ wèi shénme bù chuān yī jiàn wàitào?
7. Nǐ kěyǐ bāng wǒ de máng ma?
8. Wǒ kěbùkěyǐ mǎi zhè tiáo wéijīn?

C.2.a. Text translation to English:

Zhàoměi: What is this?

Máodì: This is an overcoat.

Zhàoměi: What is this?

Máodì: This is a pair of pants.

Zhàoměi: Are you going to China?

Máodì: Yes. Because it is winter now in China, therefore I will take winter clothes.

Zhàoměi: In winter time, is it cold in China?

Máodì: In winter time, it is cold in Beijing. Wind, rain, snow – you got it all. I have to carry with me a scarf and a pair of warm socks. I also have to buy luggage.

Zhàoměi: When do you want to go to China?

Máodì: Tomorrow, I will go to China.

Zhàoměi: Would you like me to help you with your things?

Máodì: Why would you like to help me?

Zhàoměi: Because you are my friend, therefore I would like to help you!

Máodì: You simply are a very good friend.

Zhàoměi: No... where where??

C.2.b. Questions about the text:

1. Míngtiān Máodì qù Zhōngguó.

2. Máodì fàng le yī tiáo wéijīn, yī shuāng nuǎn de wàzi.

3. Yīnwèi Zhàoměi shì Máodì de péngyǒu.

Chapter 6

Do You Have Room Service in Your Hotel?

A. Vocabulary

Times		Daily Phrases	
Wǎn	Evening; Late	Wǒ xiǎng yào...	I would like to...
		Gěi nǐ...	Here you go...
Nouns		Zhù yī wǎn	To stay one night
Jiǔdiàn	High-level hotel	Bùhǎoyìsi	How embarrassing; Excuse me
Bīnguǎn	Standard hotel	Bùkèqi	Your welcome; It's okay, no need to be so polite
Dàtáng	Lobby		
Lǚyóutuán	Tourist group	**Verbs**	
Dǎoyóu	Tourist guide		
Qiántái	(Hotel) Reception	Huàn	To exchange; To change
Zìdòng	Automatic	Rùzhù	To check-in (at a hotel)
Fútī	Stairs	Tuìfáng	To check out
Zìdòng fútī	Escalator	Méiyǒu	There isn't

Nouns		Verbs	
Bīnkè	Hotel guest	Fù	To pay
Zhèngjiàn	Documents; Papers	Wàng	To forget
Xínglǐ	Suitcase or Luggage content	Xiǎng	To wish; To want
Xínglǐxiāng	Luggage's case	Děi	Must; To have to
Kèfáng	(Guest) Room	Yòng	To use
Fúwù	Service	Zuò	To do
Kèfáng fúwù	Room service	Shuō (huà)	To talk (words)
Cāntīng	Dining room	Yào	To want; To need
Yóuyǒng	To swim		
Chí	Pond; Pool		
Yóuyǒngchí	Swimming pool	Adverbs	
Qián	Money		
Yājīn	Deposit	Zhǐ	Only
Wèishēng	Hygiene	Duō	Many
Zhǐ	Paper	Háishi	Or (for question form)
Wèishēngzhǐ	Toilet paper	Huòzhě	Or (For positive and negative sentence forms)
Cèsuǒ / Xǐshǒujiān	Toilet	Dāngrán	Of course
Hùzhào	Passport	Zhǐyǒu…, cái…	Only if there is…, only then…

121

Kělè	Cola	Zhǐyào..., jiù...	If only there is (one of this)..., then...
Yàoshi	Keys		
Dānrén	Single (person)		
Shuāngrén	Double (person)		
Fángjiān	Room	Lǐ	In; Inside
Dānrénfáng	Single room		
Shuāngrénfáng	Double room	Xiàng	Towards; To
Wēndù	Temperature		
Zǎofàn	Breakfast		
Biànxié	Slippers	Question words	
Diànshì	TV		
Céng	Floor	Wéi	"Hello?" (at the phone)
Hào	Number (of a room; of a date etc.)	Duōshǎo?	How much?
Fànguǎn	Restaurant	Zěnme yàng?	How is it?; How is it going?
Xiānsheng	Mr.; Sir	Nǎr / Nǎ lǐ?	Where?
Numbers		Measure words	
Líng	Zero	Jiān	MW for rooms
Yāo	One (for room number; phone	Píng	MW for bottles

	number; bus line number etc.)	
	Measure words	
	Hú	MW for pots

B. Grammar

1. The phrase "Xiǎng yào"

This phrase is composed of two words – 'thinking' and 'want.' Together, they form an expression or a phrase of the meaning "thinking about wanting something" or "thinking about wanting to do something." This phrase is a polite way of the verb 'yào' ('to want'). Usually, we will use this phrase in public places such as a hotel or a restaurant.

2. The phrase "Zhíyǒu…, cái…" and "Zhǐyào…, jiù…"

The phrase "Zhǐyǒu…, cái…" is composed of two parts. **'zhǐ'** means 'only' and **'yǒu'** means 'there is' and together they form the phrase **"there's only."** **'Cái'** means **"only then…"** - this phrase is a conditional type of phrase which shows that a person must fulfill a

"must require condition"; otherwise, the whole situation is not possible. It means that there are no other ways the situation could occur.

The phrase *"Zhǐyào…, jiù…"* to the contrary, means that as long as a person will perform **at least one condition from a set of conditions**, the situation **could take place**. It means that there are some other ways that this situation will be possible. The word **'Jiù,'** among other meanings, here means **'then'**.

Ex. 1. *"Zhǐyǒu* hē chá, *cái* kuài lè." ----------> "One must drink tea and only then will he become happy." This phrase actually means that if we drink tea, we will be happy, as a single option that must be followed.

Ex. 2. *"Zhǐyào* shuō Zhōngwén, *jiù* kěyǐ le." ----------> Means "As long as you will speak Chinese, then it will be fine" (There are more ways to make the situation possible, but this way is a sufficient one).

3. The phrase "Gěi nǐ"

This phrase is a polite way of saying, "here you go," like in English. It emphasizes the gesture and being helpful.

4. The use of 'Děi'

The adverb 'děi' (meaning 'must') shows a situation where an action must be done. 'Děi' could also be a verb meaning 'need' when an action needs to be done immediately without any delay.

5. The conjunction word 'Huòzhě'

'Huòzhě' functions as a word that expresses an option between two choices or between two possibilities. It is the word for 'or' in **positive** and **negative** sentences.

6. The phrase "Zhù yī wǎn"

This phrase is used to express a night stay in a hospitality place. While you check-in to a hotel, you will need to notify the reception clerk how many days you will be staying. Therefore "yī wǎn" literally means "one evening," whereas it actually means "one night (of staying)." The word zhù here is 'to live,' but here, it functions as 'to stay.' So if you would like to stay 2 nights, for example, you will need to say "wǒ xiǎng zhù liǎng wǎn." ----------> "I would like to stay (for) two nights.".

C. Exercises

Practicing vocabulary with grammar:

C.1. Dialogue translation (Ch ---> En)

Please read and translate (the dialogue between a **hotel receptionist** and a **hotel guest** who just entered the lobby and would like to book a room for the night:

Bīnkè: Nǐ hǎo, wǒ xiǎng yào rùzhù. Qǐng gěi wǒ yī jiān dānrénfáng.

Jiēdài yuán: Jīntiān wǒmen méiyǒu dānrénfáng. Wǒmen zhǐyǒu liǎng jiān shuāngrénfáng. Nǐ yào ma?

Bīnkè: Hǎo, qǐng gěi wǒ yī jiān shuāngrénfáng. Nǐmén yǒu méiyǒu yóuyǒngchí?

Jiēdài yuán: Wǒmen yǒu hěn hǎo de yóuyǒngchí, shuǐ de wēndù yě bù tài lěng. Xiānsheng, Qǐng gěi wǒ nǐ de hùzhào.

Bīnkè: Gěi nǐ wǒ de hùzhào.

Jiēdài yuán: Qǐng, zhè shì nǐ de kèfáng yàoshi.

Bīnkè: Nǐmén yǒu kèfáng fúwù ma?

Jiēdài yuán: Yǒu.

Bīnkè: Bùhǎoyìsi, wǒ děi qù cèsuǒ! Cèsuǒ zài nǎr?

Jiēdài yuán: Cèsuǒ zài èr céng huòzhě kèfáng lǐ.

Bīnkè: Zhù yī wǎn shì duōshǎo qián?

Jiēdài yuán: Zhù yī wǎn 150 kuài qián.

Bīnkè: Hǎo, Xièxie nín.

Jiēdài yuán: Bù kèqi.

_____

_____

_____

_____

_____

_____

_____

_____

_____

_____

_____

_____

_____

_____

_____

_____

_____

C.2. Questions about the dialogue

Please answer the following questions in **Chinese** regarding the dialogue above:

1. Bīnkè xiǎng yào **shénme yàng** (what kind of) de kèfáng?

_____

_____

_____

_____

_____

2. Qiántái xiàng bīnkè yào le shénme zhèngjiàn?

_____

_____

_____

_____

3. Jiǔdiàn yóuyǒngchí shuǐ de wēndù zěnme yàng?

_____

_____

_____

_____

C.3. Sentences translation

Please translate the following sentences from English to Chinese:

1. Hi, where is the hotel reception?

   _____

2. Tomorrow, I think I will do a Check-in. Do you have a single room to give me?

   _____

   _____

3. Hello, I am a tourist guide. I would like 5 rooms for two guests and 2 single rooms.

   _____

   _____

4. Tomorrow, you can go to the swimming pool and go to the dining room to eat breakfast.

   _____

   _____

   _____

5. Where is the elevator?

   _____

   _____

6. Hello? Is this room service? I would like to have one bottle of Cola and two bowls of noodles, please. Thank you.

_____

_____

_____

_____

_____

7. I have to talk with the tour guide, where is he?

_____

8. Please hand me your passport, Sir.

_____

9. There are no towels in my room.

_____

10. I forgot my room keys.

_____

11. There is one pair of socks in my luggage, two pairs of black pants and one blue shirt.

_____

_____

_____

_____

_____

12. There is no Toilet paper in my room.

_____

13. Your room is on the 5th floor, room number 1501.

_____

14. I need to do check-out. How much money do I need to pay?

_____

_____

_____

_____

15. Can I use cash or only Credit Card to pay?

_____

C.4. Filling in the missing details

Please write down in Chinese what you **have** and what you **don't have** in your hotel room, so that the housekeeper will take care of it:

Méiyǒu zài kèfáng	**Yǒu** zài kèfáng
1. Kèfáng lǐ **méiyǒu** wèishēngzhǐ.	1. Kèfáng lǐ **yǒu** máojīn.
2. _____	2. _____
3. _____	3. _____

D. Chapter summary

In this chapter, we went over a lot of vocabulary and grammar points, more than usual. This chapter is important <u>for planning to travel to China for a short duration of time or for a</u> longer time.

E. The culture corner

Staying in a hotel in China

While staying at a hotel in China, you will be surprised to experience the following: **First**, in most cases, you will have to give your passport to the receptionist and you will get it only after half an hour, more or less. This is very common in China in registering inside or outside tourists, especially foreigners. You will receive the passport to your room. The Chinese must register you at the local government system that you are located in this place in addition to your regular check-in procedure in any hotel worldwide, such as name, home address registration, etc.

Secondly, you will find out that at the dining room in your hotel, in most cases, it doesn't matter which rank it is or how many stars it has, there will always be the basic food Chinese people like and used to, such as dumplings, dian xin, different types of rice and some hot vegetables.

Thirdly, in most cases, there are no English speakers in the reception in standard hotels in China with 4-5 stars ranks. There is a crew of approximately 5-6 English speakers in luxury and well-known brands hotels at any time or in any shift. So what do you do in case you don't have English speakers in the reception? Well, that's why we are here to learn Basic Mandarin, after all.

Picture 8: A nice lobby in a standard Chinese Hotel in China.

Answers for chapter 6

C.1. Dialogue translation (Ch ---> En)

Guest: Hello, I would like to check-in. Please give me a single room.

Receptionist: Today, we don't have single rooms. We only have 2 double rooms. Would you like one?

Guest: Ok, please give me one double room. Do you have a swimming pool?

Receptionist: we have a very good swimming pool, the water temperature is also not too cold. Please hand me your passport, Sir.

Guest: Here you go.

Receptionist: Please, this is your room key.

Guest: Do you have room service here?

Receptionist: We have.

Guest: Oh, excuse me. I have to go to the WC! Where is the WC?

Receptionist: The WC is located on the second floor or inside your room, of course.

Guest: how much is it to stay one night?

Receptionist: one-night stay is 150 Yuan.

Guest: Ok, thank you.

Receptionist: You welcome.

C.2. Questions about the dialogue

1. Bīnkè xiǎng yào yī jiān dānrénfáng.

2. Qiántái xiàng bīnkè yào le hùzhào.

3. Jiǔdiàn de yóuyǒngchí shì hěn hǎo de yóuyǒngchí. Shuǐ de wēndù yě bù tài lěng.

C.3. Sentences translation

1. Nǐhǎo, jiǔdiàn de qiántái zài nǎ lǐ?

2. Míngtiān wǒ xiǎng rùzhù. Nǐmén yǒu méiyǒu dānrénfáng gěi wǒ?

3. Nínhǎo, wǒ shì Dǎoyóu. Wǒ xiǎng yào wǔ jiān shuāngrénfáng hé liǎng jiān dānrénfáng.

4. Míngtiān nǐ kěyǐ qù yóuyǒngchí yě kěyǐ qù cāntīng chī zǎofàn.

5. Diàntī zài nǎlǐ ne?

6. Wéi? Zhe4 shì kèfáng fúwù ma? Qǐng gěi wǒ yī píng kělè hé liǎng wǎn miàntiáo. Xièxie.

7. Wǒ děi hé dǎoyóu shuōhuà, tā zài nǎr?

8. Xiānsheng, qǐng gěi wǒ nǐ de hùzhào.

9. Wǒ de kèfáng méiyǒu máojīn.

10. Wǒ wàng le wǒ de kèfáng yàoshi.

11. Zài wǒ de xínglǐxiāng yǒu yī shuāng wàzi, liǎng tiáo hēisè de kùzi hé yī jiàn lánsè de chènshān.

12. Wǒ de kèfáng méiyǒu wèishēngzhǐ.

13. Nǐ de kèfáng zài wǔ céng, yāo wǔ líng yāo hào.

14. Wǒ děi rùzhù. Wǒ yào fù duōshǎo qián?

15. Wǒ kěyǐ yòng xiànjīn háishi zhǐ yòng xìnyòngkǎ fù qián?

C.4. Filling in the missing details

Méiyǒu zài kèfáng	Yǒu zài kèfáng
1. Kèfáng lǐ **méiyǒu** wèishēngzhǐ.	1. Kèfáng lǐ **yǒu** máojīn.
2. Kèfáng lǐ **méiyǒu** yī píng shuǐ.	2. Kèfáng lǐ **yǒu** yī hú chá.
3. Kèfáng lǐ **méiyǒu** yī shuāng biànxié.	3. Kèfáng lǐ **yǒu** diànshi.

Chapter 7

How Much Does This Shirt Costs?

A. Vocabulary

Nouns		Verbs	
Miànbāo	Bread	Mǎi	To buy
Niúnǎi	Milk	Mài	To sell
Jīdàn	Egg	Mǎimài	Business (transactions)
Yóu	Oil	Kàn	To look; To read; To visit; To think
Jiàngyóu	Soy sauce	Kǎn	To chop; To cut down
Shìchǎng	Market	Jiàgé	Price
Chāoshì	Supermarket	Kǎnjià	To bargain
Chéngzhī	Orange juice	Fù	To pay
Shǒubiǎo	Hand watch	Wán	To complete (an action)
Lǐngdài	Necktie	Dǎsuàn	To plan; To intend
Ěrhuán	Earrings	Zhīdào	To know
Yǎnjìng	Eyeglasses	Wéi	To wear (by wrapping around)
Qípáo	Cheongsam (traditional Chinese dress)		
Wéijīn	Scarf		

Nouns

Dōngxi	Things
Chī de	Things for eating
Hē de	Things for drinking
Gòuwù	Shopping
Zhōngxīn	Center
Gòuwù zhōngxīn	Shopping center
Chǎnpǐn	Products
Zhìliàng	Quality
Shòuhuòyuán	Shop assistant
Cháyè	Tea leaves

Verb complement

Dào	To succeed in reaching the result of an action

Sentence particles

Děng děng	Et cetera
Le	Completed action; New situation; Past tense
Ne	Softening the sentence particle; elliptic question particle
Huì	Will (future tense)

Fù		MW for pairs and sets of things (glasses)
Kuài		MW for pieces of cloth

Adverbs

Yìqǐ	Together
Xiān	First; Before
Zài	Again; Then
Jiù	Then
Hái	Still
Yī xià	All at once; A bit (to try)

Conditionals

Yàoshi	If

Common phrases

Bǐfāng shuō	For example
Huì zěnme zuò	Will be doing

Prepositions

Zhīhòu	Right after
Gēn	With

B. Grammar

1. The phrase "Bǐfāng shuō."

The phrase "Bǐfāng shuō" means "for example," It is used after talking about some topic that you would like to give examples on. Its use is relatively like in English grammar.

Example:

Wǒ xǐhuān shuǐguǒ, bǐfāng shuō xīguā, pútáo hé xiāngjiāo.

I like fruits, for example, watermelons, grapes and bananas.

2. The word particle, "Děng děng."

This particle is like 'etc.' in English. It will also be at the end of the sentence.

Example: Wǒ xǐhuān shuǐguǒ, bǐfāng shuō xīguā, pútáo, xiāngjiāo děng děng.

I like fruits, for example: watermelons, grapes, bananas, etc.

3. "Zài...lǐ..." location sentence pattern

This pattern sentence is composed of 'zài' and 'lǐ,' which means 'at (some place)' and 'inside' respectively.

For example, if I would like to say that I am inside the restaurant drinking tea, I will say: "Wǒ zài cānguǎn lǐ hē chá."

The structure will be as followed:

zài + location + lǐ

4. Result complement

Result complement is a part of the sentence which talks about **some action with a result**.

For example:

The action ----> eating   the result -----> to complete (eating).

Therefore, the **result complement** will be -------> complete eating.

For this complement of "finish eating" (the word to complete is **'wán'**), we add the "completed action le" that we have learned before (because 'le' actually represents a new situation of the eating process ---> which is **finishing** the food).

We will then have this structure:

$$\boxed{\text{Subject } + \text{ verb } + \textbf{wán} + \text{le}}$$

5. "xiān…, zài…" sentence pattern

The "xiān…, zài…" sentence pattern is coming to say to us that <u>there is some sequencing of action</u>, one in the beginning and the other will be later on.

For example:

In Chinese PinYin: Wǒ xiān chī le fàn, zài hē le shuǐ.
This means: At first, I ate (some) rice, then I drank (some) water.

6. Complex sentences structure

This is basically a long sentence that contains some basic and advanced structures (like sentence pattern type).

As a new learner, when we reach this level of sentence, we are already handling common and standard speaking structures in Mandarin Chinese of everyday life. It is when we can connect another sentence like this and already have a paragraph! By this, we can actually start to convey towards the recipient some more

144

interesting and advanced messages, which are not only "hello, how are you" and "I ate rice."

Example:

"Yīnwèi wǒ de hǎo péngyou lái Zhōngguó, suǒyǐ wǒ xiān qù kàn tā, zài hé tā yìqǐ qù jiǔdiàn de cāntīng chī wǎnfàn."

"Because my good friend comes to China, therefore, first I will go to see her, then we will go together to the hotel's dining room to eat dinner."

So you can see in the example above how much grammar we used here and the sentence is one sentence and a very long one, relatively speaking.

7. The special word particle 'ne'

This 'ne' particle has many uses, but we will only elaborate on **2 main functions**:

a. Softening the sentence – When asking questions about doing things or about some location, it can sometimes be considered rude just by asking directly. For example, "what are you doing?" or "where are you?". Chinese people are preventing this direct manner of approach in their culture or at least are trying as much as possible to

145

soften it a bit. Therefore, using the particle 'ne,' when located at the very end of this kind of direct question, helps Chinese people to make their questions or queries softer and friendlier with its tone and atmosphere. The 'ne' particle can sometimes be translated to English as "I wonder what...".

Examples:

1. "Wéi? Nǐ zài nǎr ne?"

   (Which means: "Hello? (I wonder) where are you?")

2. "Xiǎo lǐ, wǒmén děi zǒu le. Ni zuò shénme ne?

   (Which means: "Xiao li, we have to go. (I wonder) What are you doing?")

b. Creating an "Elliptic Question" – when person A asks person B a question, for example, person B answers. Now, suppose person B wants to ask the same question and wants to return the question to person A without repeating the question. In that case, Person B will use 'ne' in the question "nǐ ne?" as in the meaning of "and what about you (regarding this question)?"

Example:

Person A: Nǐhǎo, nǐ Jīntiān zài Gòuwù Zhōngxīn dǎsuàn mǎi shénme?

("Hello, what are you planning to buy today at the shopping center?")

Person B: Dǎsuàn mǎi liǎng shuāng piàoliàng

de kuàizi. Nǐ ne?

("I plan to buy two pairs of beautiful chopsticks.

What about you? ")

Person A: Hái bù zhīdào.

("I still don't know.")

* As you can see, the arrow represents person A question returned to him by person B without B repeating this question. The arrow has an elliptic kind of shape, and that's why it is called the "elliptic question" 'ne.'

8. The special adverb 'Yī Xià'

'Yīxià' is a **special adverb** because it comes after a verb and not before it, like we are used to seeing already. The sense it gives to the verb is a sense of trying a bit of the action, or to do the action at once, pretty quickly.

Example: "Wǒ xiǎng kàn yī xià."   (Means: "I think of looking (at it) and to try it a bit.")

147

9. The **VO** (Verb+Object) of 'Kǎnjià' (to bargain)

This VO of 'Kǎnjià' is exactly one of the VO's we have mentioned before that can be split up (the verb and the object split up from each other). We can put an adverb in the middle of this VO phrase, such as 'Yīxià.' The result will be "Kǎn yīxià jià," which means "To bargain a bit."

10. The complement of an action using 'Dào'

When we note that someone did an action and succeeded by reaching the result he/she wanted (or not), we use 'Dào' as a compliment.

Structure:

> Subject + Verb + Dào + Object

For example: "Wǒ zhǎo (= to look for) dào le tā."

Meaning: "I was managed to look after him and to find

him (eventually)".

C. Exercises

Practicing vocabulary with grammar:

C.1. Dialogue translation – Please read the dialogue and try
to translate it:

Zhàoměi: Nǐ hǎo ma? Wǒ jīntiān zǎoshàng yào qù chāoshì mǎi dōngxi.
Chāoshì zěnme zǒu?

Máodì: Nǐ yīzhí zǒu, zhīhòu dì èr gè lùkǒu yòu zhuǎn, chāoshì jiùzài nǐ
de zuǒbiān.

Zhàoměi: Xièxie. Yīnwèi zài jiā wǒ méiyǒu chī de, suǒyǐ zài chāoshì lǐ
wǒ děi mǎi hěn duō chī de dōngxi, bǐfāng shuō miànbāo, dàngāo,
bǐnggān, jīdàn děng děng. Zài chāoshì lǐ mǎi wán le zhīhòu, wǒ qù
Běijīng Gòuwù Zhōngxīn, nàr wǒ yě dǎsuàn mǎi dōngxi. Nǐ yào bú yào
gēn wǒ yìqǐ qù?

Máodì: Hǎo, xíng. Nǐ xiǎng mǎi shénme ne?

Zhàoměi: Wǒ xiǎng mǎi yī kuài shǒubiǎo, yī fù yǎnjìng, yī jiàn qípáo,
děng děng. Yàoshi chǎnpǐn de zhìliàng hǎo, wǒ jiù xiān gēn
shòuhuòyuán kàn yīxià jià, zài fù qián.

149

C.2. Questions about the dialogue

Please answer the following questions in Chinese regarding the dialogue:

1. Jīntiān zǎoshàng Zhàoměi zài chāoshì lǐ yào mǎi shénme ne?

_____

_____

_____

_____

2. Chāoshì lǐ mǎi wán le zhīhòu, Zhàoměi qù Nǎr?

_____

_____

_____

3. Zhàoměi zài Běijīng gòuwù zhōngxīn lǐ dǎsuàn zuò shénme?

_____

_____

_____

4. Yàoshi chǎnpǐn de zhìliàng hǎo, Zhàoměi huì zěnme zuò?

_____

_____

_____

_____

C.3. Sentences reorganization

Please organize the words and phrases into sentences like in example 1:

1.   méiyǒu, chī de, zài, jiā, wǒ, lǐ, dōngxi.

---->   Zài jiā lǐ wǒ méiyǒu chī de dōngxi.

2.   wǒ, mǎi, míngtiān, xiǎng, 10 (shí), jīdàn, gè.

---->

_____

3.   jiù,   shǒubiǎo,   yī kuài,   yàoshì,   qù,   wǒ,   Gòuwù Zhōngxīn, dǎsuàn mǎi.

---->

_____

D. Chapter summary

So in this chapter, we have learned a few advanced grammar points, some nice shopping vocabulary, and some good practice. In the next chapter, we will summarize chapters 4-7. We will also do a thorough revision of these chapters' vocabulary and grammar points, so stay tuned.

E. The culture corner

Nánjīng road in Shànghǎi, China

The Nánjīng road in Shànghǎi city is one of the most beautiful and main roads in urban China, both for locals and foreigners. As one can notice, the architecture along the road consists of European architecture imported by the settlers that came to Shanghai in the 19th century. You can also buy different products that can be luxury and pretty expensive in the grand stores with brands from all over the globe, consisting of Chinese and western brands. You can also cross the road on foot and a nice local tram at a symbolic price. In general, this road is only one of many amazing sites in Shanghai city. Many people view "a must-see Mega-City in China" for Western tourists who travel in the grand, magnificent China.

Picture 9: "Nánjīng Lù" (literally: "Nanjing Road"), China. This amazing road or avenue is attracting many tourists from all over China and all over the world. The size, the lights, the atmosphere of modern versus the ancient, the vibes – all of these make this road to be one of the most famous and special streets around the world.

Answers to chapter 7

C.1. Dialogue translation

Zhàoměi: How are you? Today, in the morning, I would like to go to the supermarket to buy things. How can I go to the supermarket?

Máodì: You go straight, after it, in the second intersection you turn right, the supermarket is just on your left side.

Zhàoměi: Thank you. Because I don't have things to eat at home, therefore, inside the supermarket, I have to buy a lot of food, for example, bread, cake, cookies, eggs, etc. After I finish buying my things inside the supermarket, I will go to Beijing's Shopping Center; I also plan to buy things there. Do you want to come with me or not?

Máodì: Ok, sure. What would you like to buy?

Zhàoměi: I am thinking of buying one pair of gloves, one eyeglass, one Cheongsam (Traditional Chinese Dress), etc. If the product quality is good, I will first bargain a bit with the salesman and then pay the money.

C.2. Questions about the dialogue

1. Jīntiān zǎoshàng Zhàoměi zài chāoshì lǐ yào mǎi dōngxi. Bǐfāng shuō miànbāo, dàngāo, bǐnggān, děng děng.

2. Zhàoměi qù Běijīng Gòuwù Zhōngxīn.

3. Zhàoměi zài Běijīng Gòuwù Zhōngxīn lǐ yě dǎsuàn mǎi dōngxi.
Bǐfāng shuō yī kuài shǒubiǎo, yī fù yǎnjìng, yī jiàn qípáo, děng děng.

4. Yàoshi chǎnpǐn de zhìliàng hǎo, Zhàoměi jiù Dǎsuàn xiān gēn
shòuhuòyuán kàn yīxià jià, zài fù qián.

C.3. Sentences reorganization

2. wǒ, mǎi, míngtiān, xiǎng, 10 (shí), jīdàn, gè.

----> Míngtiān wǒ xiǎng mǎi shí gè jīdàn.

3. jiù, shǒubiǎo, yī gè, yàoshì, qù, wǒ, Gòuwù Zhōngxīn,
dǎsuàn mǎi.

----> Wǒ yàoshi qù Gòuwù Zhōngxīn, jiù dǎsuàn mǎi yī kuài shǒubiǎo.

Revision on Chapters 4 - 7

A. Vocabulary summary

Verbs		Times	
Zǒu	To step to; To walk to	Yǐhòu	After
Guǎi	To turn to	Yǐqián	Before
Zhuǎn	To turn to	Zhīhòu	Right after (an action)
Yǒu	To have	Zhīqián	Right before (an action)
Xiǎng	To think (about doing something); To miss (someone)		

Nouns		Daily phrases	
Lǐ	Inside		
		Qǐngwèn	Excuse me…; I would like to ask, please…
Bīnguǎn	Hotel		
Lù	Way		
Kǒu	Mouth	Jiùshì	Simply is…; Really is…
		Jiùzài	Is just at…

Colors

Nouns

		Yánsè	Color
Lùkǒu	Intersection		
Jiā	Home; Family	Hóngsè	Red
Dēng	Light	Lǜsè	Green
Jiē	Street	Hēisè	Black
Hónglǜdēng	Traffic light	Huángsè	Yellow
Diàn	Electricity	Lánsè	Blue
Yǐng	Shadow	Fěnsè	Pink
Diànyǐng	Movie	Huīsè	Grey
Yuàn	Courtyard	Zǐsè	Purple
Diànyǐngyuàn	Cinema	Chéngsè	Orange
Yínháng	Bank		

Adverbs

Jiù	Then; Just	Yòu	Right
Děi	Must to; Have to	Zuǒ	Left
Hái	Still	Yīzhí	Straight
		Biān	Side
		Duìmiàn	In front of

Directions

Prepositions

Lǐ	In
Wǎng	To (somewhere)

Question words

Zěnme?	How?; How to?
Nǎr? / Nǎ lǐ?	Where?

Measure

Auxiliary

words

Jiā	MW for Buildings and businesses

words

Dì	Auxiliary word for ordinal numbers (**the** first, **the** second, **the** third...)

Numbers

Sì	Four
Wǔ	Five
Liù	Six
Qī	Seven
Bā	Eight
Jiǔ	Nine
Shí	Ten
Shíyī	Eleven
Shíèr	Twelve
Shísān	Thirteen
Èrshí	Twenty
Yībǎi	One hundred

Times

Zuótiān	Yesterday
Míngtiān	Tomorrow
Nián	Year
Qùnián	Last year
Míngnián	Next year
Xīngqi / Lǐbài	Week
Yuè	Month
Xiàtiān	Summer

Nouns

Yīfú	Cloths
Dàyī	Overcoat
Wàzi	Sock
Wéijīn	Scarf
Xínglǐ	Luggage
Màozi	Hat
Chènshān	Shirt
Kùzi	Pants

Qiūtiān	Autumn	Huā	Flower
Dōngtiān	Winter	Shù	Tree
Chūntiān	Spring	Tàiyáng	Sun
		Yǔ	Rain
		Xuě	Snow
		Fēng	Wing

Pronouns

Zhè; Zhèi (gè)	This / This one		
Nà; Nèi (gè)	That / That one		

Verbs

Hěn	To be (comes before an adjective)

Adjectives

Xíng	Okay	Dài	To take; To carry
Lěng	Cold	Mǎi	To buy
		Chuān	To wear
Rè	Hot	Dài	To put on
Nuǎn	Warm	Bāng (máng)	To help (with someone's matters)
Yīntiān	Cloudy day	Xūyào	Must; Have to; Need to
Qíngtiān	Sunny day	Dào	To arrive to; To go to
Qiángliè	Intense		

Question words

Shénme?	What?; Which?

Adverbs

Hĕn	Very	Wèi shénme?	Why?
Tài	Too much	Shénme shíhou?	When?
Zhēn	Really; Truly		

<u>Measure words</u>

<u>Prepositions</u>

Jiàn	MW for upper wear	Cóng	From
Tiáo	MW for pants		
Dĭng	MW for hats		

<u>Sentence particles</u>

	Le	Particle of status complement; Past tense particle

<u>Times</u>

<u>Daily Phrases</u>

Wăn	Evening; Late	Wŏ xiăng yào...	I would like to...
		Gĕi nĭ...	Here you go...

161

Nouns

Jiǔdiàn	High-level hotel
Bīnguǎn	Standard hotel
Dàtáng	Lobby
Lǚyóutuán	Tourist group
Dǎoyóu	Tourist guide
Qiántái	(Hotel) Reception
Zìdòng	Automatic
Fútī	Stairs
Zìdòng fútī	Escalator

Zhù yī wǎn	To stay one night
Bùhǎoyìsi	How embarrassing; Excuse me
Bùkèqi	Your welcome; It's okay, no need to be so polite

Verbs

Huàn	To exchange; To change
Rùzhù	To check-in (at a hotel)
Tuìfáng	To check out
Méiyǒu	There isn't

Nouns

Bīnkè	Hotel guest
Zhèngjiàn	Documents; Papers
Xínglǐ	Suitcase or Luggage content
Xínglǐxiāng	Luggage's case
Kèfáng	(Guest) Room
Fúwù	Service
Kèfáng fúwù	Room service

Verbs

Fù	To pay
Wàng	To forget
Xiǎng	To wish; To want
Děi	Must; To have to
Yòng	To use
Zuò	To do
Shuō (huà)	To talk (words)

Cāntīng	Dining room	Yào	To want; To need
Yóuyǒng	To swim		
Chí	Pond; Pool		
Yóuyǒngchí	Swimming pool	Adverbs	
Qián	Money		
Yājīn	Deposit	Zhǐ	Only
Wèishēng	Hygiene	Duō	Many
Zhǐ	Paper	Háishi	Or (for question form)
Wèishēngzhǐ	Toilet paper	Huòzhě	Or (For positive and negative sentence forms)
Cèsuǒ / Xǐshǒujiān	Toilet	Dāngrán	Of course
Hùzhào	Passport	Zhǐyǒu…, cái…	Only if there is…, only then…
Kělè	Cola	Zhǐyào…, jiù…	If only there is (one of this)…, then…
Yàoshi	Keys		
Dānrén	Single (person)		
Shuāngrén	Double (person)	Prepositions	
Fángjiān	Room	Lǐ	In; Inside
Dānrénfáng	Single room		
Shuāngrénfáng	Double room	Xiàng	Towards; To
Wēndù	Temperature		

163

Zǎofàn	Breakfast	Question words	
Biànxié	Slippers		
Diànshì	TV		
Céng	Floor	Wéi	"Hello?" (at the phone)
Hào	Number (of a room; of a date etc.)	Duōshǎo?	How much?
Fànguǎn	Restaurant	Zěnme yàng?	How is it?; How is it going?
Xiānsheng	Mr.; Sir	Nǎr / Nǎ lǐ?	Where?

Numbers		Measure words	
Líng	Zero	Jiān	MW for rooms
Yāo	One (for room number; phone number; bus line number etc.)	Píng	MW for bottles
		Measure words	
		Hú	MW for pots

Nouns		Verbs	
Miànbāo	Bread	Mǎi	To buy

164

Niúnǎi	Milk	Mài	To sell
Jīdàn	Egg	Mǎimài	Business (transactions)
Yóu	Oil	Kàn	To look; To read; To visit; To think
Jiàngyóu	Soy sauce	Kǎn	To chop; To cut down
Shìchǎng	Market	Jiàgé	Price
Chāoshì	Supermarket	Kǎnjià	To bargain
Chéngzhī	Orange juice	Fù	To pay
Shǒubiǎo	Hand watch	Wán	To complete (an action)
Lǐngdài	Necktie	Dǎsuàn	To plan; To intend
Ěrhuán	Earrings	Zhīdào	To know
Yǎnjìng	Eyeglasses	Wéi	To wear (by wrapping around)
Qípáo	Cheongsam (traditional Chinese dress)		
Wéijīn	Scarf		

Verb complement

Nouns

		Dào	To succeed in reaching the result of an action
Dōngxi	Things		
Chī de	Things for eating		
Hē de	Things for drinking		

Gòuwù	Shopping		

		Sentence particles	
Zhōngxīn	Center		
		Děng děng	Et cetera
Gòuwù zhōngxīn	Shopping center	Le	Completed action; New situation; Past tense
Chǎnpǐn	Products	Ne	Softening the sentence particle; elliptic question particle
Zhìliàng	Quality	Huì	Will (future tense)
Shòuhuòyuán	Shop assistant		
Cháyè	Tea leaves		

		Measure words	
		Fù	MW for pairs and sets of things (glasses)
		Kuài	MW for pieces of cloth

Yìqǐ	Together		
Xiān	First; Before	Conditionals	
Zài	Again; Then	Yàoshi	If
Jiù	Then		
Hái	Still		
Yī xià	All at once; A bit (to try)		
		Common phrases	
Prepositions			
		Bǐfāng shuō	For example
Zhīhòu	Right after	Huì zěnme zuò	Will be doing
Gēn	With		

B. Grammar points summary

1. The expression "Qǐngwèn"

- <u>Structure:</u> * "Qǐngwèn, ...?"

167

2. WH Questions

- The WH questions are, "Where?" "When?" "How?" "How much?" "Why?" "What?" "Who?", "Which?", etc.
- **In most cases will replace the WH Question itself**

3. Counting objects with " Dì."

- <u>Structure</u>:

$$Dì + number$$

4. Changing Direction formula

- <u>Structure</u>:

$$Wǎng \ + \ zuǒ / yòu \ + \ zhuǎn / guǎi$$

5. The expression "how to go to (somewhere)?" - "zěnme zǒu?"

- <u>Structure</u>: Location + zěnme zǒu?

6. The pronouns zhè; zhèi and nà; nèi

- 'Zhè' **is** 'this'; 'Nà' **is** 'that'

7. The use of 'hěn' with adjectives as the verb 'to be'

- When we use the adverb 'hěn' in a simple sentence with an adjective, we use it like the verb **"to be"** (am; is; are).

8. The Predicate-Adjective type of sentence

- Structure:

> Subject + Adverb + Adjective

9. The phrase "Please help me with my business/issues" --> "Qǐng bāng wǒ de máng."

- "Qǐng bang wǒ de máng" is a phrase that is built from Verb+Object kind of verb, or in short --------> VO.

10. Past tense le; New situation le

- "Past tense le" Structure:

> Subject + verb + le + (object)

- "New situation le" Structure:

> Subject + verb/Adj. .... + le

11. The phrase "Xiǎng yào."

- "Thinking about wanting something" / "Would like to..."

12. The phrase "Zhíyǒu…, cái…" and "Zhǐyào…, jiù…"

- "Zhǐyǒu…, cái…" ------> Shows that a person must fulfill a **"must require condition,"** otherwise the whole situation is not possible.

- "Zhǐyào…, jiù…" ------> Means that as long as a person will perform **at least one condition from a set of conditions**, the situation **could take place**.

13. The phrase "Gěi nǐ"

- This phrase is a polite way of saying, "here you go," like in English. It emphasizes the gesture of being helpful.

14. The use of 'Děi'

- The adverb 'Děi' (means 'must') shows a situation where an action must be done.

15. The conjunction word 'Huòzhě'

- 'Huòzhě' (means 'or') functions as a word that expresses an option between two choices. Appears in positive and negative sentences.

16. The phrase "Zhù yī wǎn"

- "Zhù yī wǎn" is a phrase that is being used to express a night stay in a hospitality place (means "To stay one night").

17. The phrase "Bǐfāng shuō"

- The phrase "Bǐfāng shuō" means "for example" and It is used after talking about some topic that you would like to give examples on.

18. The word particle "Děng děng"

- This particle is like 'etc.' in English.
- Will also be at the end of the sentence.

19. "zài...lǐ..." location sentence pattern

Structure:

zài + location + lǐ

20. Result complement

- Result complement is a part of the sentence which talks about **some action with a result**.

- Structure:

> Subject + verb + **wán** + le

21. "Xiān…, zài…" sentence pattern

- The "Xiān…, zài…" sentence pattern expresses a sequence of action.

22. Complex sentences structure

- This is basically a long sentence that contains some basic and some advanced structures.

23. The special word particle 'ne'

- a. Softening the sentence – When asking questions about doing things or about some location, it can sometimes be considered rude just by asking directly.

- b. Creating an "Elliptic Question" – When a person wants to ask the same question someone asked him but would not like to repeat the whole question.

24. The special adverb 'Yī xià'

- Comes after a verb.

- Gives the verb a sense of **"trying a bit"** (of the action) or doing it **at once**.

25. The **VO** (**V**erb + **O**bject) of 'Kǎnjià' (to bargain)

- A **"Verb + Object"** type of verb.
- **V + O** Can be split. For example, in the phrase: **"Kǎn yīxià jià"**, 'Yi xià' is added, and the whole phrase means "To bargain a bit."

26. The complement of an action using 'Dào.'

- Structure:

> Subject + Verb + Dào + Object

C. Exercises

C.1. Translation Practice sentences (makes perfect!)

* Ch -------> En Translation

1. Qǐngwèn, "chūntiān fànguǎn" zěnme zǒu?

_____

2. Nǐhǎo! Wǒ shì zhè gè lǚyóutuán de dǎoyóu.

_____

3. Nǐmén zài jiǔdiàn lǐ yǒu diàntī ma?

_____

4. Zài <u>zhè lǐ</u> (here) wǒ kěyǐ huàn qián ma?

_____

* EN -------> Ch Translation

1. I would like to buy a lot of blue shirts.

_____

2. Hi! I would like to do check-in please.

_____

3. In my room, there is no toilet paper.

_____

4. Tomorrow morning, I will go to the supermarket to buy stuffs like bread, cake, etc.

_____

_____

5. Inside the shopping center, I'm thinking about buying a green coat and one pair of blue pants.

_____

_____

C.2. Sentences reorganization

Please organize the words and phrases into sentences like in **example 1**:

1. Qípáo, yào, mǎi, wǒ, liǎng, jiàn.

-----> Wǒ yào mǎi liǎng jiàn qípáo.

     (Meaning: I would like to buy 2 cheongsam)

2. Yàoshì, wǒ, míngtiān, Zhōngguó, qù, jiù, děi, wǒ, xínglǐxiāng, mǎi, Yī xiāng.

----->

_____

_____

3. Lǐ, xínglǐ, zài, wǒ, dǐng, yī, yǒu, maòzi.

----->

_____

4. .De shíhou, xiàtiān, rè, hěn.

----->

_____

5. Dōngtiān, chuān, .de shíhou, tā, wéijīn.

----->

_____

6. Wèishénme, tā, yī dǐng, dài, méi, màozi?, <u>xiǎng dào</u> (thought).

----->

_____

7. <u>Person A:</u>   Děi, wǒ, cèsuǒ, qù.

   Zěnme, cèsuǒ, zǒu?.

   ----->

   _____

   _____

8. Wǎnshàng, jīntiān, xiān, wǒ, kàn, yīnyuè, shū, zài, tīng,
dǎsuàn.

   ----->

   _____

   _____

9. Lái, jiā?, wǒ, nǐ, shénme shíhou.

   ----->

   _____

C.3. Picture description

Please describe in a few sentences the following pictures. You will be assisted by the example given in the first picture. **Some new words are <u>underlined,</u> and their meaning is inside the brackets after them.**

First Picture

<u>Zhàopiàn</u> (photo) lǐ de <u>rénmen</u> (People) shì Zhōngguórén. Tāmén zài <u>Qiánmén jiē</u> (Qianmen street) zǒu lù (walking in the road). Tāmén chuān wàitào, Yī gè rén chuān hēisè de wàitào, <u>qítā</u> (other) de rén

chuān zōngsè (brown color) de wàitào, dài yī dǐng (measure word for hats) màozi. Yīnwèi xiànzài shì dōngtiān, tiānqì (the weather) zhēn lěng. Rénmen dàgài qù chāoshì mǎi dōngxi.

* In **the second & the third pictures**, please try to say and describe what you see with some sentences regarding the people shown in them, who they are, what they are doing, etc.

Second Picture

Answers for revision on chapters 4 - 7

C.1. Translation Practice sentences

* Ch -------> En Translation

1. Excuse me, how do I go to "Spring Restaurant"?

2. Hello! I am the tourist group's tour guide.

3. Do you have an elevator inside your hotel?

4. Can I change money in here?

* EN -------> Ch Translation

1. Wǒ xiǎng mǎi hěn duō lánsè de kùzi.

2. Nǐhǎo! Wǒ xiǎng yào rùzhù.

3. Zài wǒ de kèfáng lǐ méiyǒu wèishēngzhǐ.

4. Míngtiān zǎoshàng wǒ qù chāoshì mǎi dōngxi. Bǐfāng shuō miànbāo, dàngāo, děng děng.

5. Zài gòuwù zhōngxīn lǐ wǒ xiǎng mǎi yī jiàn lǜ sè wàitào hé yī tiáo lánsè de kùzi.

C.2. Sentences reorganization

2. -----> Wǒ yàoshi míngtiān qù Zhōngguó, wǒ jiù děi mǎi yī gè xínglǐxiāng.

3. -----> Zài xínglǐ lǐ wǒ yǒu yī dǐng màozi.

4. -----> Xiàtiān de shíhou hěn rè.

5. -----> Dōngtiān .de shíhou, tā wéi wéijīn.

6. -----> Tā wèi shénme méi xiǎng dào dài yī dǐng màozi?

7. -----> Person A: Wǒ děi qù cèsuǒ.

   Cèsuǒ Zěnme zǒu?

8. -----> Jīntiān Wǎnshàng wǒ dǎsuàn xiān kàn shū, zài tīng yīnyuè.

9. -----> Nǐ shénme shíhou lái wǒ jiā?

C.3. Picture description

* First picture description (translation to English)

The people in the photo are Chinese. They are at Qianmen Street, walking in the road. They are wearing coats. One person is wearing a black coat, (and) the other person is wearing a brown coat and a hat. This is because of winter; the weather is really cold. The people probably went to the supermarket to buy things.

** Second picture possible description in Chinese

Rénmen zài cānguǎn lǐ. Tāmén dàgài shì Zhōngguórén. Yǒu rén mǎi fàn, yě yǒu rén chī fàn. (Zài) Cānguǎn lǐ nǐ kěyǐ chī miànbāo, dàngāo hé bǐnggān. Nǐ kěyǐ hē chá hé rè shuǐ.

** Second picture possible description (translation to English)

The people are at the restaurant. Some people are buying food, and some people are eating food. Inside the restaurant, you can eat bread, cake and cookies. You can drink tea and hot water.

*** Third picture possible description in Chinese

Zhè shì yī jiā cháyè diàn. Shāngdiàn lǐ yǒu hěn duō chá. Yǒu lǜchá hé hóngchá. Zài shāngdiàn lǐ yě yǒu bǐnggān nǐ kěyǐ mǎi. Shāngdiàn yǒu liǎng céng.

*** Third picture possible description (translation to English):

This is a tea store. Inside the store, there are many tea (types). There is green tea and red tea. Inside the tea store, there are also cookies you can buy. The store has 2 floors.

Chapter 8

Traveling with public transportation in China

A. Vocabulary

Times		Nouns	
Rì	Day	Chē	Car
Yuè	Month	Dìtú	Map
		Piào	Ticket
		Jīngjù	Beijing Opera
Verbs		Zhàn	Station
		Zìxíngchē	Bicycle
Zuò	To seat; To take a ride		
Kāi	To open; To drive (a car)	Chūzūchē	Taxi
Jiào	To call (sb. or sth. as)	Gōngjiāochē	Bus
Qí	To ride	Dìtié	Subway
Dǎ	To hit; To type; To catch a taxi	Fēijī	Airplane
Jìn	To enter	Jīchǎng	Airport
Zū	To rent	Rùkǒu	Entrance
Gǎnxiè	To thank	Chūkǒu	Exit
		Shūdiàn	Book store
		Kuài	Piece of money
Adverbs		Fēn	Penny
		Qiánmén	Qianmen street
yěxǔ	Maybe		
		Fēnzhōng	Minutes
		Tīng	Hall

Jǐ?; Jǐ gè?	How much? (for small numbers; for asking about family members)

Measure words

Directions

		Liàng	MW for vehicles
Dān	Single; One way		
Chéng	Trip	Kuài	MW for money and currency units
Dānchéng	One way trip	Bān	MW for groups
Wǎng	To go (in a direction)	Zhāng	MW for flat items
Fǎn	To return		
Wǎng fǎn	Round trip		
Biān	Side		
Pángbiān	Next to; Beside		

B. Grammar

1. Asking for today's date

When asking for today's date, we will use the next formula:

Jǐ yuè jǐ hào? -------> jǐ (how much?) yuè (month) jǐ (how much) hào (number)

The answer to this question will be with today's month and day, and they will replace the first "jǐ" and second "jǐ" respectively.

Ex: **Xiǎo lǐ**: "Dàwèi, Jīntiān jǐ yuè jǐ hào?"

("David, Which date is it today?")

Dàwèi: "Jīntiān wǔ yuè shí hào/rì*." ("Today is May 10th.")

* 'Rì' means day, so you can use it too instead of 'hào' when answering for today's date.

2. Question form "verb + bù + verb"

Another way of asking questions is to repeat the verb with the negation particle of 'bù' ('no') in the middle. When using this kind of question, <u>there is no need for the regular question particle of 'ma' at the end of the sentence.</u>

Ex: <u>Xiǎo Ding:</u> "Xiǎo lǐ, nǐ yào bù yào hé wǒ pǎobù?

("Xiǎo lǐ, would you like or not like to have

a run with me?")

3. Financial expressions

Financial expression refers to the times we need to ask or say something related to money or a sum of money. The measure word of money is 'kuài' and means 'piece' – means, piece of money.

Usually, we will say "8 Yuán" (Yuán or Rénmínbì is the currency in China, as US Dollar is the currency of USA) as "bā kuài" or "bā kuài qián" which means "8 pieces (of Yuan)" or "8 pieces (of) money (of Yuan)" respectively. You can choose which one of them to use; both are ok.

Below are some world currencies (1) and Chinese money units (2).

a. Some world currencies

1 Chinese Yuan --------------------> 1 Yuán

1 American Dollar ------------> 1 Měiyuán

1 Japanese Yen -----------------> 1 Rìyuán

1 European Euro --------------> 1 Ōuyuán

b. Money Units

1 kuài/Yuán------------> 1 Yuán (100% of Yuán)

1 máo/jiǎo ----------> 0.10 Yuán (10% of Yuán)

1 fēn ------------------> 0.01 Yuán (1% of Yuán)

c. Chinese money units - examples

• 3 Yuan ----------------------> Sān kuài / Sān kuài qián

• 2 dime (of Yuan) -------------------> Liǎng máo (Yuán)

• 5 cents (of Yuan) ----------------------> Wǔ fēn (Yuán)

C. Exercises

C.1.a. Text

Màikè (Mike): Qǐngwèn, Jīntiān jǐ yuè jǐ hào?

Huáng mǐn: Jīntiān sì yuè sān rì.

Màikè (Mike): Xièxie nín. Nín zhīdào bù zhīdào dìtiězhàn zài nǎlǐ?

Huáng mǐn: Nǐ kàn, dìtiězhàn de rùkǒu zài wǒmén de duìmiàn.

Màikè (Mike): Xièxie. Nín yěxǔ zhīdào wǒ zài nǎlǐ kěyǐ mǎi Běijīng de dìtú?

Huáng mǐn: Nǐ yīzhí zǒu, dì èr gè lùkǒu yòu zhuǎn. Shūdiàn jiùzài nǐ de yòubiān. Zài shūdiànlǐ nǐ kěyǐ mǎi Běijīng de dìtú.

Màikè (Mike): Hǎo, wǒ zhēn de gǎnxiè nín. Zàijiàn.

Huáng mǐn: Bù yòng xiè. Zàijiàn.

C.1.b Text questions – True / False

Please circle the correct answer:

a. The tourist is speaking with a local Chinese Citizen. (True / False)

b. The tourist wants to rent a car. (True / False)

c. The tourist wants to reach the nearest subway station. (True / False)

d. The tourist wants to buy a map of Shanghai. (True / False)

e. The tourist is rude. (True / False)

f. The tourist is polite. (True / False)

D. The culture corner

Transportation in China

In China's main cities, such as Beijing, Shanghai, Chengdu, Tianjin, Guangzhou, and Shenzhen, the transportation infrastructure is well built. This is due to the massive population getting bigger and bigger inside cities each year, which causes the country to plan and deploy grand-sized infrastructure projects appropriately. It is very convenient to go by Subway, as for a few Yuans, one could cross the entire city from east to west or from north to south.

The buses and taxies in the cities, such as in Shenzhen, are starting to be "green" by going on electricity or hybrid – combining fuel and electricity together. You can still see many bicycles but not the amounts you would see a few decades ago in the '70s or the '80s.

Besides that, there are also "bullet" trains (extra high-speed trains) which reach up to 217 mph (!!!) between cities, and usually, tickets are relatively cheap. Transportation in China offers various means to deal with the population's size.

In rush hours, you still need to be extra patient. The rush hours are mainly 7:30 am-9:30 am, and in the afternoon, it is usually 4:30 pm – 7:30 pm. It is a great experience to travel in China whether by Taxi, Bus, Subway or your local Chinese friend's car.

Picture 10: A daily trip inside a subway in Shenzhen, China. The metro in China's major cities is very clean, safe, modern and user friendly. Traveling inside the subway at Shenzhen for example, is a very good experience and it is very safe, even at late hours.

Answers to Chapter 8

C.1.b Text questions – True / False

a. True

b. False

c. True

d. False

e. False

f. True

What Have We Learned & Looking Ahead

Here, we are in the end of this study book of Mandarin Chinese for beginners. It is the end of the start of our journey together to the wonderful world of Chinese civilization and culture in general and the mystery of the Chinese language in particular.

We have accomplished the first step, which is the basic knowledge about China's most spoken dialect called Mandarin. We saw that the language grammar structure is modular and "Lego" like. We also noticed some simple rules for starting making a sentence in Chinese language, forming a paragraph, until creating a short passage, and all of these in a relative short time.

The vocabulary we went through in this book was pretty vast and diverse and gave us a glimpse and a taste of the most basic aspects the Chinese language can be about. **We have practiced** much of the new vocabulary and grammar shown during the chapters we have studied and were getting to know much better the **Chinese world of thought**.

Nevertheless, there is more knowledge to gather about this unique and wonderful language, especially the <u>written language</u> discussed in the second study book. The book will include, among the rest, some basic knowledge about the Chinese writing system, the difference between Traditional and Simplified Characters, the structure and the design of the Chinese characters, the cultural thought behind the writing, pictograms and ideograms and much more interesting stuff.

At the end of this book, if so, we can have some "Small Talks" with new Chinese friends or some Chinese work colleagues, and we can also understand better the thinking and the rhythm behind the spoken language. We were introduced to a whole new aspect of

Chinese unique language feature, which is the four tones in Mandarin.

I do hope you could make the most of the knowledge you acquired through this study book. I wish to see you in the coming books, which will give a wider perspective and a more comprehensive understanding of this magnificent language.

About the Author

The 21st century is the century in which China is getting stronger economically & culturally, influencing much of the western world's rhythm and trends. The importance of Chinese as a mediate language in our small "global village" was never much important as it today.

Shachar Deutsch graduated from Tel-Aviv University in East-Asian Studies and Geography and saw the importance of making the Chinese language more accessible to the western world by making this language relatively easy to grasp and introduce.

Today, after living in China for some time and experiencing advanced Chinese language courses in Shenzhen, China, Shachar works nights and days to make the Chinese language learning methods more attractive and simple to start and learn in the long run.

Among the many new and creative ways to grasp the extraordinary "Chinese treasures" hiding inside the Chinese language, Spoken and written language, there is much work being done by Shachar to find many new ways and methods to learn the language more efficiently and in other ways than being taught today.

After travelling to China many times, including living there for some time, new ideas and perspectives are being expressed uniquely in his new books.

Made in the USA
Monee, IL
26 May 2023